MAPPING
THE
UNIVERSE

MAPPING THE UNIVERSE

Exploring and chronicling the cosmos

ANNE ROONEY

ARCTURUS

ARCTURUS

This edition published in 2017 by Arcturus Publishing Limited
26/27 Bickels Yard, 151–153 Bermondsey Street,
London SE1 3HA

ISBN: 978-1-78428-538-8
AD005420UK

Printed in China

Contents

INTO THE VOID

'For there is a single general space, a single vast immensity which we may freely call Void; in it are innumerable globes like this one on which we live and grow. This space we declare to be infinite, since neither reason, convenience, possibility, sense-perception nor nature assign to it a limit. In it are an infinity of worlds of the same kind as our own.'

Giordano Bruno, *On the Infinite Universe and Worlds* (1584)

OUR DISTANT ANCESTORS SAW MANY MORE stars than we can make out in our light-polluted skies, perhaps prompting the urge to investigate and map the heavens. Some of the earliest surviving archaeological structures seem to have been used to track the movement of the Sun and Moon or to be aligned with certain stars. The earliest written records provide evidence of people tracking the planets and mapping the stars.

AREAS GREAT AND SMALL

Terrestrial and celestial maps have developed in opposite directions. Terrestrial maps were first made for very localized areas, covering the distance a person could travel on foot or by horse or boat. As civilizations advanced, exploring further afield, so did the extents of their maps. The pattern of astronomical mapping has been the opposite of this. The entire sky has been immediately visible through all time, but details of the Moon and planets only emerged with the development of the telescope, and later still with space travel. The larger picture has also grown bigger and more complex. More objects have emerged from the darkness as we have improved our optical telescopes and developed instruments which can look at the sky in different ways, detecting other types of electromagnetic radiation.

MODELLING THE HEAVENS

Just as terrestrial maps reflect social, political, scientific and philosophical positions, so maps of the heavens embody different beliefs and mental models. Records of astronomical events and observations date back thousands of years, but they have generally come down to us without any theoretical cosmological context. The earliest para-scientific cosmological theories were left by the Ancient Greeks around 2,500 years ago. The Greeks were the first to develop models of the universe based in philosophy rather than mythology and religious belief. Their suggestions included an infinite universe, with other worlds, a solar system centred on the Sun and, conversely, a world system with Earth at the centre of the universe.

This fresco, known as the 'Star of Ghassul', was found in the ruins of a house in the Jordan valley and is 6,000 years old. (This is a computer-enhanced image.)

A broken slab of limestone found at the site of the ruined Tal Qadi temple in Malta might represent a map of the heavens 5–6,000 years old. It is thought to show the sky divided into five portions with stars and a crescent moon.

The last of these was the one which prevailed, being supported by the philosopher Aristotle in the 4th century BC and developed mathematically by the Egyptian astronomer Ptolemy in the 2nd century AD. From the Classical world it was transmitted to the Arab lands of North Africa and eventually back to Europe, where it went unchallenged until the 16th century. The Christian Church helped to sustain the geocentric (Earth-centred) model. It fitted well with the notion that God had created the universe and put it in motion for the benefit of humankind, and that it was unchanging and perfect. Unfortunately, the model was wrong.

The great paradigm shift in astronomy came in 1543, with the publication of a new model by the Polish astronomer Nicolaus Copernicus, which put the Sun at the centre of the solar system. The change also gave the universe a chance to leak out into boundless space, no longer neatly contained and kept in order by God. The map of the universe had to be redrawn – though it took more than two centuries before the new model was accepted by the majority of astronomers (and the Church).

LOOKING AND LEARNING

The next great change came only a few decades after Copernicus died, with the invention of the telescope in 1609. Immediately, it yielded surprising revelations. The planets resolved into discs, no longer just spots of light – but the stars remained points. The Moon had a rugged, imperfect surface. Some of the planets had moons of their own. And the Milky Way was revealed as a band of stars, uncountable and astonishing. More mapping opportunities arose, as astronomers could record the surfaces of the planets and the Moon, and map stars that had previously been invisible.

Telescopes improved, bringing more and more of the universe into focus. Around 200 years ago, in the early 1800s, scientists discovered that light from the Sun (and later other stars) has a spectral 'fingerprint' which can reveal the chemical composition and temperature of the body producing the light. Spectroscopy became a vital tool in astronomy. The 20th century added the radio telescope and then other types of telescope and detector to the astronomer's toolbox, offering further ways of investigating and mapping the heavens. And, in the second half of the 20th century, space travel took us the next step. Now telescopes in space, orbiters and planetary landers can map planets and moons of the solar system in detail which would have been unimaginable to the astronomers of the early modern age.

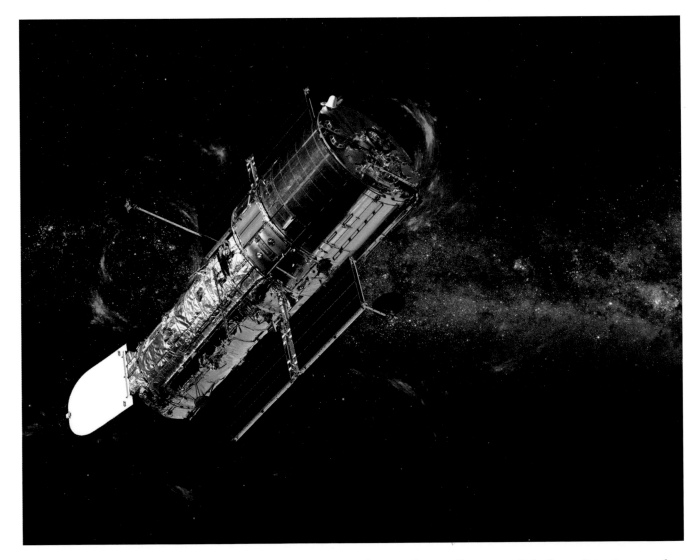

Telescopes sited in space are unhampered by Earth's atmosphere and can collect more light from distant areas of the universe than any Earth-based device.

OBSERVING TOGETHER
Although technology has made mapping the universe easier, our ancestors were not devoid of tools to help them. Observatories dedicated to watching, recording and measuring the movements and positions of the celestial bodies sprang up in China, then India and the Middle East, and later Europe. They were equipped with tools and professional astronomers, serving rulers by providing information essential to maintaining the calendar and predicting celestial movements and events.

Astronomers use a variety of instruments in the observatory of the astronomer Taqi al-Din in Constantinople, 16th century.

NAKED-EYE MAPPING

The principal early instruments were the armillary sphere, the quadrant and the sextant.

The armillary sphere was used by Arab and medieval astronomers to measure the location of objects in the sky using a coordinate system based on the ecliptic (the apparent path of the Sun across the sky). It consists of a central globe representing the Earth and a framework of rings representing important lines such as the ecliptic, the celestial equator and the meridians. The sphere was set up for the observer's latitude by aligning the fixed meridian ring North–South, perpendicular to the horizon. Its orientation was set by sighting the Sun or a star of known celestial longitude (the position on the ecliptic). Other objects could then be sighted and their coordinates read from the appropriate rings. Early versions of the armillary sphere arose independently in Ancient China and Ancient Greece; it was developed considerably by Arab astronomers.

The quadrant and sextant were like portions of a protractor. The quadrant covered a quarter of a circle, while the sextant covered a sixth. They were used with a sighting rod or slit to measure the angle of elevation of a celestial object. They could be small, hand-held instruments or so large that they were built into the fabric of an observatory.

With these instruments, and later with telescopes, astronomers have mapped the positions of the stars in our own galaxy, the Milky Way.

Turkish astronomers using a large armillary sphere, 16th century.

ASTRONOMY AND ASTROLOGY

Today we think of mapping the universe as the work of astronomers, and linking celestial events with human lives the province of astrologers. In the past there was less or no distinction between astronomy and astrology. The early Chinese astronomers mapped the stars to discover and, if they were lucky, predict unusual astronomical events; these were believed to have significance on Earth, presaging disasters and changes. Even until the late Renaissance in Europe, astronomy and astrology went hand-in-hand, with some of the great astronomers providing astrological services to rulers and casting horoscopes. Although we may now dismiss astrology as unscientific, it has served astronomy well in the past, providing the impetus for improved observations and mapping of the sky.

MAPPING CHALLENGES

In recent times, astronomers have been able to see beyond the stars of the Milky Way to find other galaxies and glimpse the immensity of the universe. Challenges for astronomical mapping range from the search for exoplanets (planets outside our solar system) to the macro structure of the universe. Within the solar system, we have begun to map the surface and internal characteristics of the other planets and their moons. Google Earth has expanded its remit to offer Google Moon and Google Mars – but there are a lot more worlds to map. Just as the terrestrial cartographers of the late 15th century found that there was far more land and sea on Earth to map than they at first believed, so we are discovering ever more land and space to record in the universe.

The Danish astronomer Tycho Brahe was the last great naked-eye astronomer. This mural quadrant was built into his island observatory, Uraniborg. A smaller sextant and an armillary sphere are visible through the arched windows.

THE CENTRE OF ALL THINGS

FROM PTOLEMY TO COPERNICUS

FROM AT LEAST THE TIME OF THE ANCIENT Greeks until the 16th century, the prevailing view in the Western world was that the Earth was at the centre of the cosmos and everything else revolved around it. The model was promoted by the Greek philosopher Aristotle and popularized by the Greek-Egyptian astronomer Claudius Ptolemy in his *Almagest*. This was the principal astronomical text, from its composition in the 2nd century AD until the 1600s, ensuring that the geocentric model dominated astronomy for around 2,000 years.

A UNIVERSAL EMBRACE

As far as we can tell, the earliest Assyrian and Egyptian models of the cosmos presented a series of bands in a domed, box- or cylinder-shaped universe. This placed the netherworld beneath the Earth, the atmosphere and the realm of stars above it, and one or more heavens beyond the stars. It was based in mythology rather than any scientific approach.

The Babylonian universe put Earth between three levels of heaven and an underworld. The whole system was surrounded by a celestial ocean.

Opposite: In Ancient Egyptian cosmology, the sky goddess Nut arches over the Earth, supporting the sky and its stars. This painting of Nut is from the tomb of Rameses VI, built in 1137BC.

CELESTIAL SPHERES

The Ancient Greek philosopher Anaximander (*c*.610–546 BC) was first to explain the structure of the cosmos. His account was based on observation rather than on mythology, though he was a metaphysician rather than a scientist. Anaximander took three important steps in explaining the universe, which have underpinned all thinking since:

- The celestial bodies (stars, planets, Moon) move in full circles, passing beneath the Earth as well as above it.
- The Earth floats unsupported in space.
- The celestial bodies occupy spherical planes surrounding Earth, but they are not all on the same plane – instead, there are concentric spheres centred on Earth.

Anaximander believed the Earth to be a thick disc, its diameter three times its height; we live on the top surface. He explained that the Earth does not fall through space as it is in the centre, with equal pressures from all directions. Anaximander's model was strange in that he put the stars in the plane closest to Earth, followed by the Moon, and finally the Sun farthest from Earth.

HELIOCENTRIC OR GEOCENTRIC?

Around 250–300 years later, Aristarchus of Samos (*c.*310–*c.*230BC) suggested that the Sun, not the Earth, was at the centre of the cosmos. He, too, used concentric circles or spheres and these were occupied by Earth (now spherical), the other planets and the fixed stars, which he put farthest from the Sun. Aristarchus proposed that the Earth turns on its axis once a day, orbits the Sun once a year, and that the stars are distant suns. Unfortunately, his model did not prevail and it took nearly 2,000 years for the Sun to be restored to its correct position in relation to Earth.

The influential Greek philosopher Aristotle (384–322BC) favoured a geocentric cosmos. He divided the area above Earth into two regions: one which included everything between the surface of the Earth and the orbital sphere of the Moon, and one which included the Moon and everything beyond. This second region was considered perfect and unchanging. And that, as we shall see, would eventually be the undoing of the geocentric model.

The Italian painter Giovanni di Paolo showed God creating the universe as a series of concentric rings, with the zodiac around the outside and the Earth at the centre.

PESKY PLANETS

Unfortunately, watching the movement of the planets over the course of a year doesn't support a model in which they simply go around the Earth. Instead, they seem to describe a series of loops, first going forwards, then doing a little backwards jiggle and completing a small circle before moving onwards again. Apollonius of Perga (262–190BC) suggested that each planet was in a small circular orbit called an epicycle. This epicycle itself was in orbit around the Earth. But his theory could only be made to work if the Earth was offset from the centre, which rather defeated the object.

Finally, in the 2nd century AD, the Egyptian astronomer Ptolemy refined the idea. His explanation had each planet orbiting in an epicycle, the centre of which orbits the eccentric

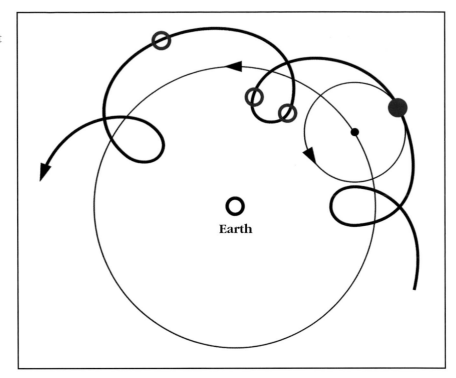

The planet (in red) goes round in its own epicycle, which in turn orbits Earth.

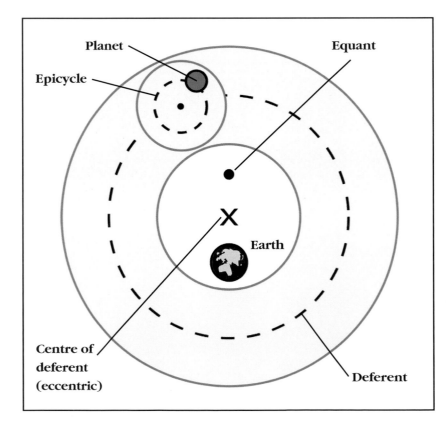

The centre of the deferent was called the eccentric – there is nothing there, it's just a point in space.

(a point in space). Ptolemy added a point opposite Earth, and an equal distance from the eccentric, which he called the equant. The planet's speed was uniform relative to the equant, so if you were able to stand at the equant and watch, the centre of the planet's epicycle would always move at the same angular speed (that is, it would cover the same angle of arc in the same period of time). This seemed a good solution as it allowed perfectly circular movement of the planets, which Aristotle required, and explained why their paths look odd from Earth. Most importantly, it could be used to predict the positions of the planets with reasonable accuracy.

Ptolemy arranged the heavenly bodies in a series of concentric crystalline spheres or 'orbs'. The Moon was closest to the Earth, followed by Mercury, Venus, the Sun, Mars, Jupiter and Saturn, with the fixed stars in an orb beyond the planets.

This manuscript illumination from the late 13th century shows the Ptolemaic system with the Sun and Moon orbiting a central Earth. Bottom left shows how a lunar eclipse is explained in this system, and bottom right shows the phases of the Moon. The circles in gold represent the crystalline spheres of the Moon and Sun; the red matter between the Earth and the Moon is fire, while beyond the Moon everything is made of aether.

REMODELLING THE COSMOS

The Ptolemaic model was finally challenged in 1543 by Nicolaus Copernicus, who proposed a heliocentric (Sun-centred) solar system in *De revolutionibus orbium coelestium* (*On the revolutions of the celestial spheres*). Copernicus had the planets in circular orbits around the Sun, but this turned out to be no more accurate than the Ptolemaic model for predicting planetary movements. There was also the distinct disadvantage that the Church didn't approve, and within 100 years had condemned the model and the teaching of it – a ban not lifted until 1758.

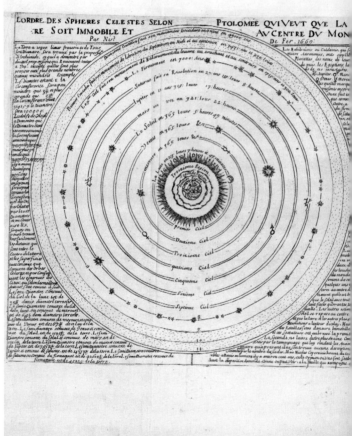

There was nothing clear from observation to discredit the Ptolemaic model. As this medieval diagram of a solar eclipse shows, celestial phenomena could be explained as easily using a geocentric model as with a heliocentric model.

The German astronomer Johannes Kepler finally developed the model of the solar system which is still current and confirmed by observations from space as well as by mathematics. In 1605, he put the planets into elliptical rather than circular orbits around the Sun, a move which immediately cleared up all the confusion about planetary motion. Even so, there was no solid evidence that his system was correct.

There were several compromise positions between the geocentric and heliocentric systems, too. Astronomers continued to argue, and astronomical cartographers continued to present all the main models as alternatives. These parallel presentations often gave the arguments for and against each system, comparing their merits and demerits in an attempt to arrive at the truth.

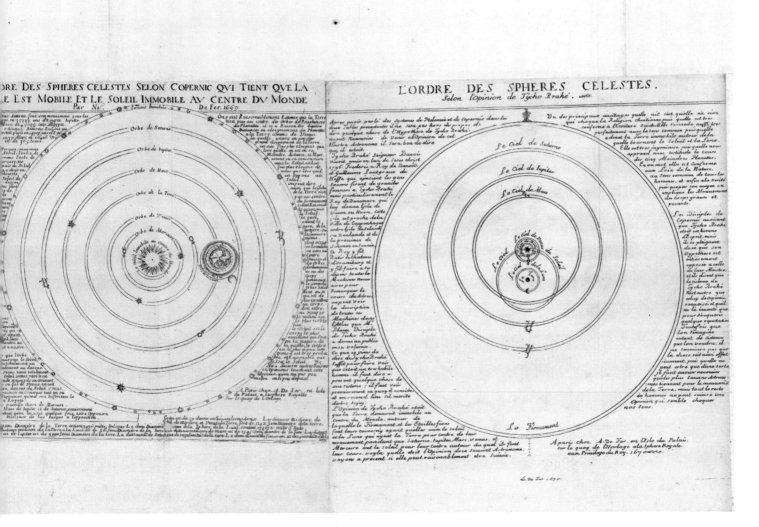

The three cosmological models of Ptolemy (left), Copernicus (centre) and Tycho Brahe (right; see page 40) as they appeared in a 1669 work by French cartographer and geographer Nicolas de Fer (1646–1720).

ARATUS, *PHAENOMENA*, 11TH CENTURY

This 11th-century French manuscript presents a Latin translation of the *Phaenomena* by Aratus, a Greek poet of the 3rd century BC. The text is a versification of a lost work by Eudoxus of Cnidus. It describes the constellations and gives only a brief and rather vague account of the planets, which Aratus says 'all pursue a shifty course', confessing 'when I come to them my daring fails'. Commentaries on Eudoxus' treatise reveal that he employed a complex scheme of multiple orbs for each of the heavenly bodies – the Moon had three orbs, for example, to account for the complexities of its movement. This illustration shows Earth at the centre, orbited first by the Moon which appears to have at least two circles. Mercury and Venus both orbit the Sun (with a fiery crown), which then revolves around the Earth. Mars, Jupiter and Saturn have their own circles. The zodiac, with figures representing the months, occupies the outer circle.

ANGELS MAKE THE WORLD GO ROUND,
BREVIARI D'AMOR, c.1300

This depiction of the Ptolemaic universe is not overly concerned with the spheres of the heavenly bodies, but shows the mechanism by which the whole is turned. The *primum mobile*, the outermost sphere which gives movement to the others, is cranked by angels using handles. In the Middle Ages, the heavenly bodies were not deemed to move themselves, but to be carried by the movement of their orb, and that was imparted from the outside of the system by the 'prime mover' (which became God, in the Christian cosmos).

The division of the Earth (at the centre) into four parts represents its supposed composition – the four Greek elements, air, fire, water and earth. The manuscript was made in the early 14th century in Provence, France, and is a verse encyclopaedia, *Breviari d'amor*, composed by Matfre Ermengaud, around 1290.

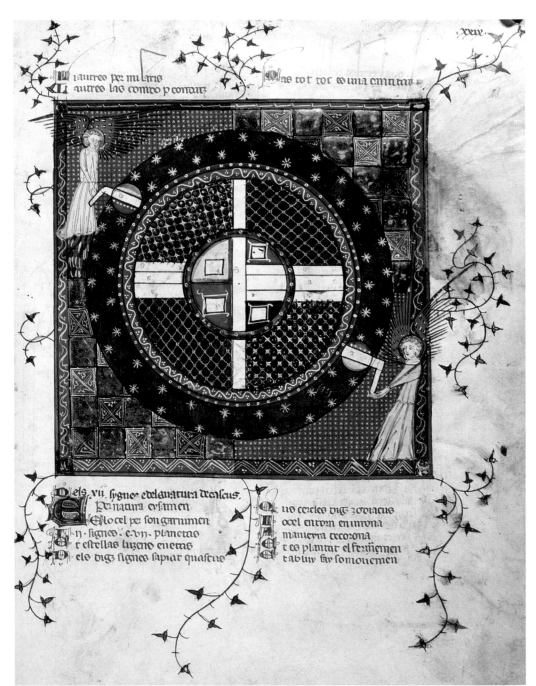

ABRAHAM CRESQUES, CATALAN ATLAS, 1375

The Catalan Atlas is perhaps the most important atlas of the Middle Ages. It consists of six long, narrow pages of vellum (parchment made from hide), possibly produced by the Jewish cartographer Abraham Cresques from Majorca. Four pages deal with the geography of Earth; the other two (shown here) depict the Ptolemaic world system.

At the centre, Earth is represented by an astronomer holding an astrolabe. This is surrounded first by circles depicting the other three of the classical elements (water, air, fire), then by the orbs of the Moon, the Sun and the five known planets. The band of the zodiac follows, which ends the cosmographic part of the diagram. The stations and phases of the Moon are shown in the next circle, followed by six rings presenting the lunar calendar and then an account of the astrological effect of the Moon when located in the different signs of the zodiac. Outside is mathematical information – the division of the circle into 360 degrees and an account of the Golden Number. Allegorical figures representing the four seasons are posted in the corners.

KONRAD VON MEGENBERG, PTOLEMAIC UNIVERSE, 1481

The usual representation of the Ptolemaic universe shows the whole scheme of orbs or spheres surrounding the Earth. It is a sort of God's-eye view from a position outside the cosmos. Konrad von Megenberg, in his *Buch der Natur* (*Book of Nature*) gave a more local perspective. Looking at just a small tract of land, the fraction of each of the spheres above it appears as a straight band, with a strip of fire directly above the earthly scene. The planets are represented in the same way as the stars – before telescopes, they could not be visually distinguished from stars. The Moon and Sun both have faces – though the Moon looks rather miserable.

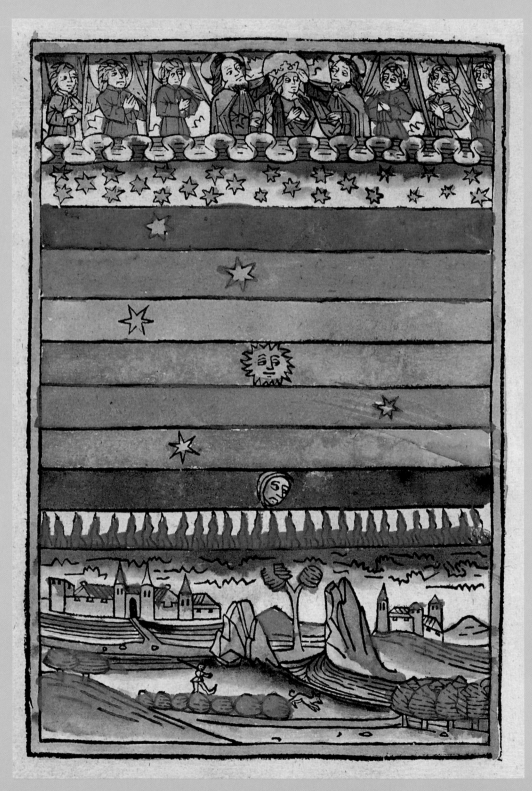

HARTMANN SCHEDEL, *NUREMBERG CHRONICLE*, 1493

The *Nuremberg Chronicle*, published in both Latin and German, was one of the first illustrated printed books. It provides a history of humankind, relying heavily on biblical narrative. This woodcut illustrates the final day of Creation, showing the Ptolemaic model of the universe in its fullest possible form.

The illustrator has added the elemental spheres at the centre, so Earth is surrounded in turn by water, air and fire, before we get to the celestial spheres. Beyond the sphere of the fixed stars (the firmament) are the 'crystal heaven' and then the *primum mobile*. The crystal heaven was added to explain the reference in the Book of Genesis to waters above the firmament. Beyond the *primum mobile* lies the Empyrean, the mind of God, and an area occupied by different orders of angels as set out by the 13th-century theologian Thomas Aquinas.

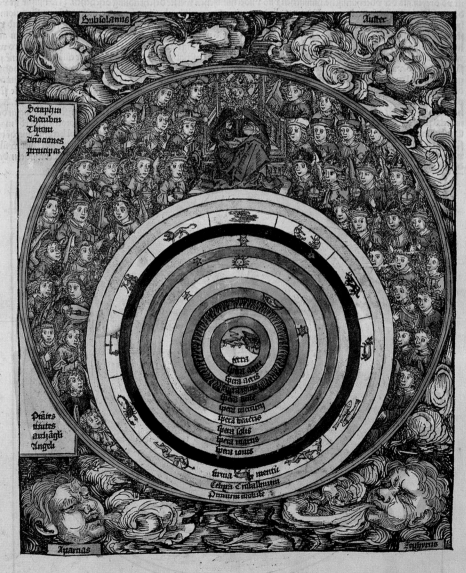

WILLIAM CUNINGHAM, ATLAS CARRYING THE HEAVENS, 1531

This illustration of Atlas carrying the Earth and heavens on his shoulders appears in *The Cosmographical Glasse, Containing the Pleasant Principles of Cosmographie, Geographie, Hydrographie,* or *Navigation* by William Cuningham. The heavens are shown in the form of an armillary sphere. The Earth is at the centre, surrounded by a spherical framework of rings representing lines of celestial longitude and latitude, the ecliptic, the celestial equator and so on.

    The framework of the armillary sphere is juxtaposed over a standard Ptolemaic map, with the Earth surrounded by air and fire, then the orbs of the Moon, Sun, planets, fixed stars, crystalline sphere and *primum mobile*. The planets are represented here by the symbols used for them in alchemical texts. There is a strange disjunction in Atlas supporting the Earth he is standing on, and the Moon and stars that are shining in the sky above him.

Hic canet errantē Lunam, Solisq̃; labores
Arcturūq̃;, pluuiasq̃; hyad. gēmosq̃; triões

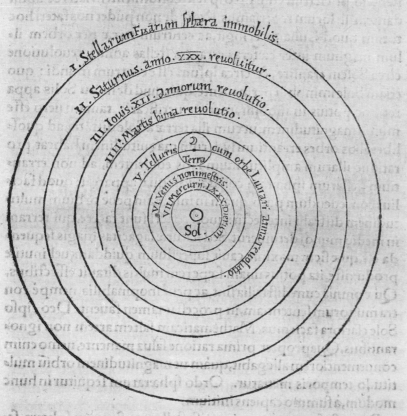

NICOLAUS COPERNICUS, THE SOLAR SYSTEM, 1543

This simple, unassuming map of the solar system marked one of the great turning points in human history. Published by Polish astronomer Nicolaus Copernicus (or Mikołaj Kopernik) in the year of his death, 1543, it overturned the Ptolemaic world system, putting the Sun at the centre with the Earth and the other planets moving around it. Copernicus probably anticipated trouble – and it came – but he was soon dead and didn't have to suffer the consequences.

Although for a while the Church tolerated the Copernican system as a mathematical and hypothetical model, once it became clear that people – including Galileo Galilei – held it as a literal representation of the form of the cosmos, the book was banned and teaching the model prohibited. Although many astronomers favoured the Copernican scheme, it was not widely adopted at first. It didn't actually produce better predictions for the movement of the planets than the Ptolemaic model, and the hostility of the Church acted against it.

Copernicus's map specifically notes that the planets, including Earth, revolve around the Sun and that the Moon orbits the Earth. The fixed stars he labels as unmoving. The other outer orbs of the Ptolemaic model have disappeared, including the bit where God was supposed to live.

BARTOLOMEU VELHO, PTOLEMAIC UNIVERSE, 1568

This cosmological map created by the Portuguese cartographer Bartolomeu Velho in 1568 shows the then-known world at the centre of the Ptolemaic universe, despite appearing 25 years after Copernicus's *De revolutionibus*.

Australasia and Antarctica are both missing from the world map, being unknown to Europeans at the time. The Sun, Moon, known planets and the fixed stars orbit the Earth, each keeping to their proper circle. The circles are marked with the orbital periods. Going out from the centre, these are: the Moon, 27 days 8 hours; Mercury, 70 days 7 hours; the Sun, 365 days; Mars, two years; Jupiter, 12 years; Saturn, 30 years; the fixed stars, 36,000 years.

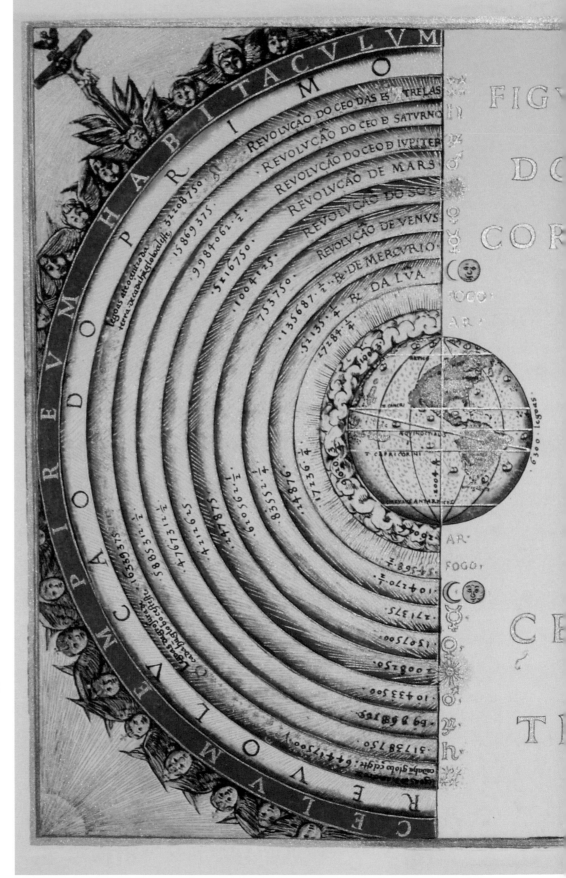

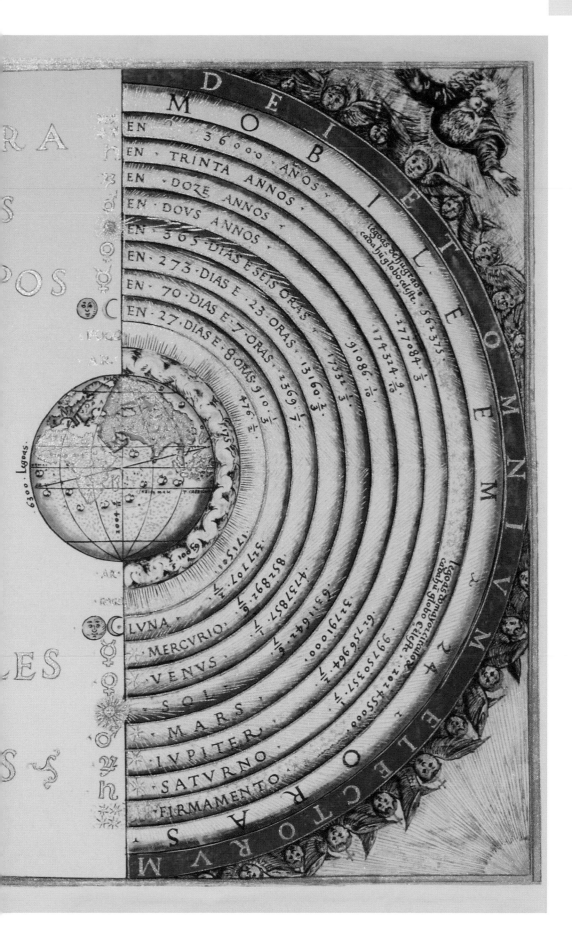

SEYYID LOQMAN ASHURI, *ZUBDAT-AL TAWARIKH*, 1583

This map comes at the start of the Turkish *Zubdat-al Tawarikh* (*Cream of Histories*) which recounts the prophet's journey into night. The first miniature in the book, it sets the scene with a cosmological map showing the Earth at the centre of the universe. It is surrounded by the seven heavens, the signs of the zodiac and the lunar mansions. Chinese, Indian and Islamic astronomy divides the path of the Moon into 28 mansions corresponding to the division of its path along the ecliptic, each representing thirteen days.

اگر زوال شد علم بنگریمکه

قال حکما اذا بصاحبی بعد

منسر برسد خاص سعد رطوبت خاک و بادند جاهن و پرو پر رز گنسته نجوشسه زرو ولیات گرد که ایت که بود زمان لگر نداد که ایا لیت الوها الرو رزگیا پ و شاکر حج چار پ زنش زارطاحمد چندد

GIOVANNI RICCIOLI, *ALMAGESTUM NOVUM*, 1651

The frontispiece to Giovanni Riccioli's *Almagestum Novum* (below) is an allegorical representation of the evaluation of two world systems, that of Copernicus and Riccioli's own amended version of the system proposed by Tycho Brahe (see page 40). Riccioli's book gives possibly the most detailed, comprehensive and considered account of the systems, maybe even excelling Galileo's seminal *Dialogue Concerning the Two Chief World Systems* of 1633, which compared the Ptolemaic and Copernican systems. Riccioli's system (shown in the balance on the right) puts Mercury, Venus and Mars in orbit around the Sun, which itself orbits the Earth, but it allows Jupiter and Saturn to orbit the Earth directly. The geocentric system of Ptolemy is shown discarded on the floor, as Riccioli considered it obsolete. The putti at the top of the image hold the planets, Sun and Moon, and a comet is included – a primary piece of evidence that Ptolemy's world system was wrong. The planets on the right are Jupiter and Saturn, with Saturn an odd shape because its rings had not yet been explained (see page 104) and Jupiter shown with stripes. The balance is tipping in favour of the Riccioli/Tycho model.

PLANISPHÆ
Sive
ORBIVM MV
HYPOTHESI
PLANO

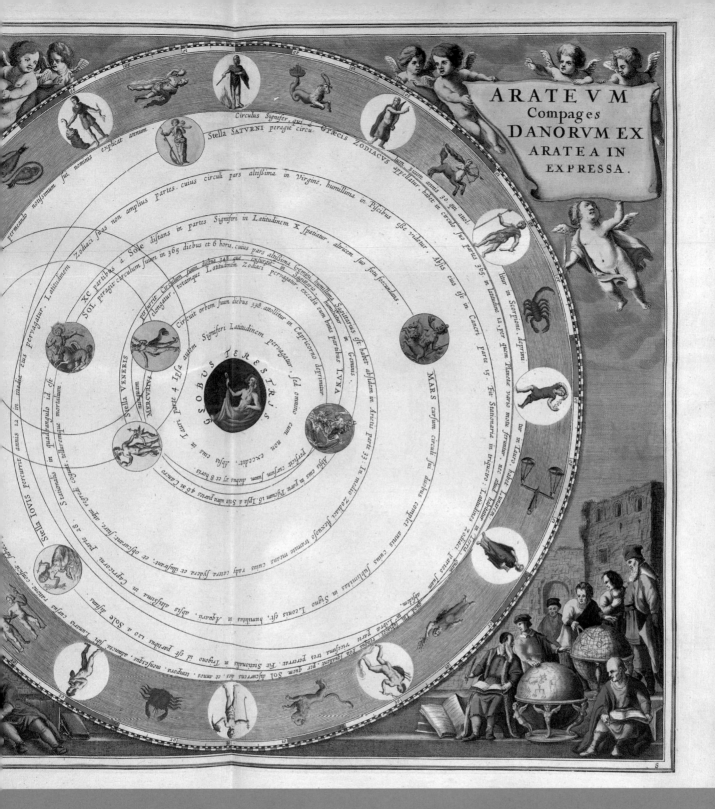

ANDREAS CELLARIUS, ARATUS PLANISPHERE, 1660

This depiction of Aratus' planisphere appeared in *Harmonia Macrocosmica*, by the German cosmographer Andreas Cellarius, first published in 1660. It is the same scheme as the one on page 25. In the lower corners, scholars study terrestrial and celestial globes. The planets are represented by images of the classical gods associated with them. *Harmonia Macrocosmica* was the final (seventh) volume of the *Chronologica*, a multi-part atlas planned by the great cartographer Gerard Mercator which was to cover all the known cosmos. Mercator died before it was completed. The first part of *Harmonia Macrocosmica* sets out the competing world systems and the second part deals with the constellations.

ANDREAS CELLARIUS, COPERNICAN PLANISPHERE, 1660

Cellarius' depiction of the solar system following the plan of Copernicus shows evidence of work with the telescope which had taken place in the intervening hundred years between Copernicus publishing his model and Cellarius his great book. Jupiter is shown with four moons, which were discovered by Galileo in 1610. Copernicus was vague about the fixed stars, and although Cellarius includes the signs of the zodiac in the outer circle, they are rather curiously surrounded by clouds.

ANDREAS CELLARIUS, TYCHO BRAHE'S WORLD SYSTEM, 1660

The Danish astronomer Tycho Brahe (1546–1601) was an eccentric yet extremely skilled astronomer based in Denmark. He built an observatory on the island of Hven in Copenhagen, where he carried out meticulous naked-eye observations. He had a metal prosthetic nose, having lost part of his own nose in a duel as a student; he also owned a pet moose, which died after drinking too much at a feast and falling down the stairs.

Tycho was aware of Copernicus's model of the solar system, but opted for something between it and Ptolemy's model. His system has the Sun, Moon and zodiac orbiting the Earth, but all the other planets orbiting the Sun. The Sun drags its entourage of planets around the Earth. Tycho found it improbable that 'Earth, that hulking, lazy body, unfit for motion' was required to move around in Copernicus's model, so allowed it to slump inert in the centre of his cosmos.

BRAHEVM,
Structura
EX HYPOTHESI
BRAHEI IN
DELINEATA.

JOHANN DOPPELMAYR, *ATLAS NOVUS COELESTIS IN QUO MUNDUS SPECTABILIS*, 1742

Johann Doppelmayr was an astronomer and cartographer, among other things. This beautiful plate from his *Atlas Novus Coelestis* depicts the state of astronomical knowledge in the early 1700s. The Sun dominates the image, lying at the heart of the Copernican model of the solar system and sending its brilliant rays out in all directions. The text gives information about the orbits and satellites of the planets. The moons of Jupiter and Saturn are shown as small stars, which is how they appeared through the telescopes of the day.

In the bottom right corner, the models of Ptolemy and Tycho Brahe are shown alongside that of Copernicus, the Copernican model being obviously preferred. The Ptolemaic planisphere is overlaid by astronomical instruments, including the telescope, indicating that technology had led to its being superseded.

The illustration bottom left shows a map of the known world, looking down from the North Pole. California is shown as an island, which was common in maps of the 17th and 18th centuries. The Sun and known planets are shown top left, with an attempt to show their relative sizes. Top right seems to show the potential existence of other solar systems amongst the clouds, which represent the universe.

PLANETARY SEQUENCE OF THE SOLAR SYSTEM, CHANDRA X-RAY OBSERVATORY, 21ST CENTURY

In *Astronomia Nova*, published in 1609, the German astronomer Johannes Kepler set out his discovery that the planets go around the Sun in elliptical orbits. Two further planets and plenty of moons, dwarf planets and other bodies have been discovered since Kepler published his findings, but they have slotted into his plan with no difficulty.

The familiar image of the solar system, compiled from photographs of our neighbours in space, shows the sequence of planets as we move out from the Sun but is deceptive in giving us no idea of scale. An image such as this one might suggest that the relative sizes of the planets are shown, but this is not the case. The problem is that the solar system is so large compared to its component parts that it would be impossible to draw a map to scale without the smaller items becoming invisibly tiny. Neither the size of the planets nor the gaps between them can be represented on an image such as this.

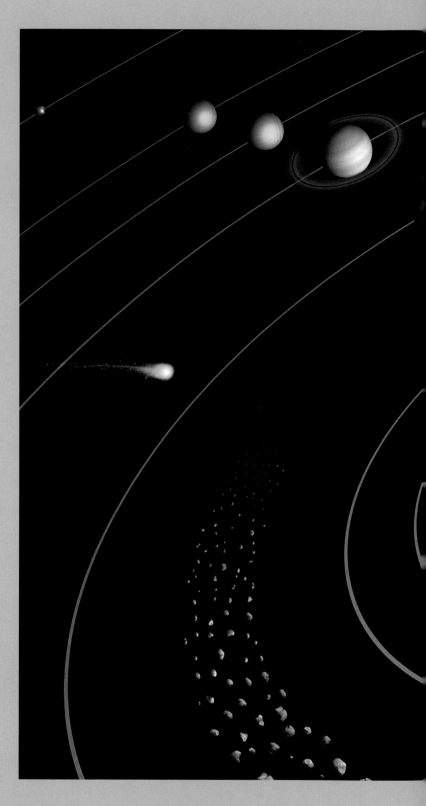

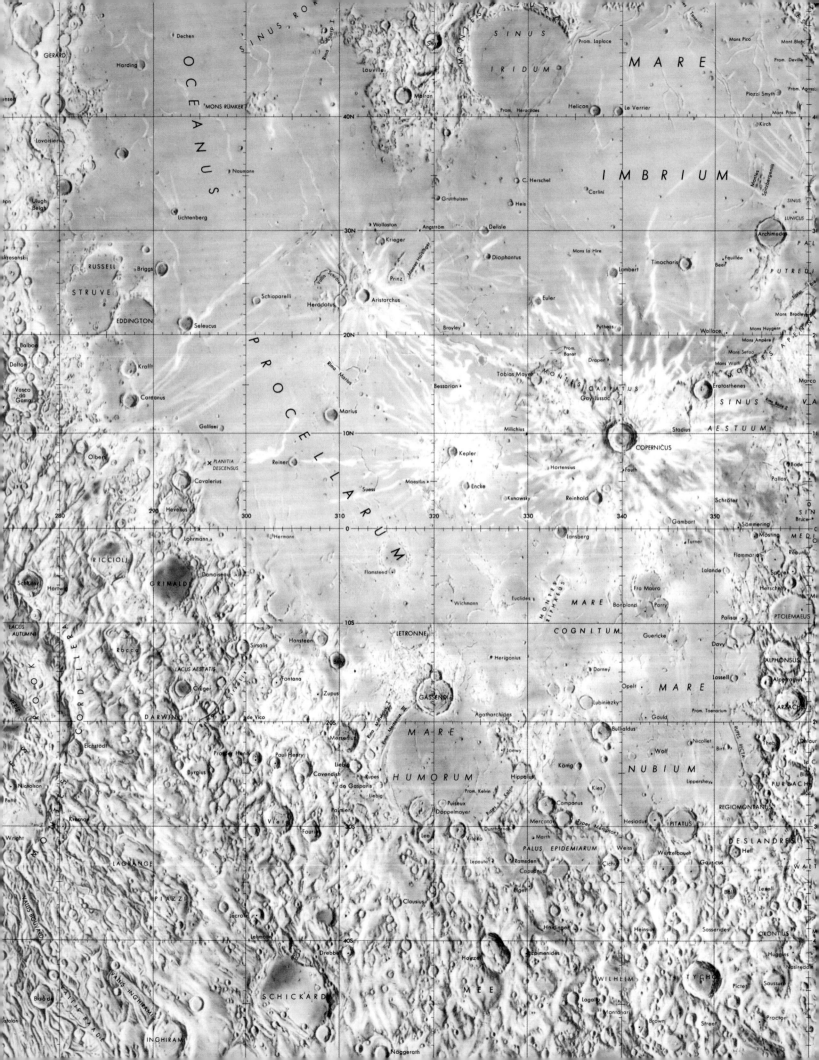

MAPPING THE MOON

OUR NATURAL SATELLITE

THE MOON WAS VISIBLE TO OUR PREHISTORIC ancestors and features in many myths, legends, stories and works of art. It was the first celestial body to be mapped and remains the most thoroughly investigated. The Moon is clearly visible to the naked eye, with regions of light and shadow that have been likened to a human face, a rabbit and an older person with a bundle of sticks. It is astonishing, then, that very few attempts to map it survive from before the 1600s. However, since the invention of the telescope 400 years ago, many people have seen and named features on the nearside of our satellite.

Until the 20th century and the advent of space travel, humans had only ever seen one side of the Moon, the nearside shown here. This shaded relief map shows the Moon from 50 degrees South to 50 degrees North.

FIRST VIEWS

The earliest known drawings of the Moon's surface are by Leonardo da Vinci (1452–1519).
He sketched the patterns of light and shadow that he saw on the Moon, illustrating his
ideas about its composition. He believed the Moon to have seas of liquid
water (dark areas) and mountains which reflected the light of the Sun. His
drawings (see example on the right) were made in his unpublished private
notebooks and remained unknown at the time.

A better-known sketch was made by the Englishman William Gilbert,
physician to Queen Elizabeth I (1540–1603), just before the advent of the
telescope in 1609. The sketch (below) wasn't published until 1651, long after
Gilbert's death. By then, more detailed images were available and his was
interesting only as a curiosity. Gilbert assumed that the dark spots he could
discern on the Moon's surface were continental landmasses, and the light
areas were seas. He noted with regret that as no one had previously drawn
the face of the Moon, it was impossible to tell whether it had ever changed.

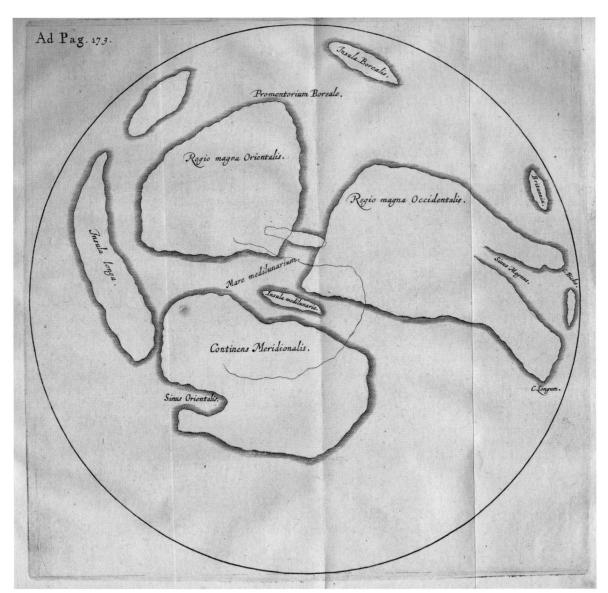

Perhaps one reason why there were few attempts to depict the Moon accurately is that it was generally believed to be featureless. This might seem to fly in the face of clearly visible evidence, but according to tradition the Moon was supposed to be perfect and unflawed. The shadows visible to the naked eye were therefore often explained away as the result of differing densities in the constitution of the Moon rather than surface imperfections. When the Moon was depicted incidentally in medieval art, it was often painted as flawless.

This crucifixion scene by the Dutch artist Jan van Eyck, painted c.1440–41, is unusual in that it shows patterning on the Moon's surface.

LUMPS AND BUMPS

The advent of the telescope put an end to all that. When magnified, the Moon very clearly had lumps and bumps. The first person to chart those lumps and bumps was English astronomer Thomas Harriot in 1609 (see page 52). More famously, Galileo used his own improved telescope to produce the first detailed images of the Moon (see page 53).

Mapping the Moon might seem an entirely academic exercise: unlike a map of the Earth, it's not going to help anyone find their way to somewhere. There is, or was until recently, no opportunity for travel over its surface or for mining or other activities that would require knowledge of the topography or geology. Yet during the first half of the 17th century mapping the Moon turned out, surprisingly, to have a very practical application. It was found that if features on the Moon could be accurately mapped and named so that the same feature could be identified by different observers, then longitudes of places on Earth could be determined from simultaneous observations during a lunar eclipse. In 1618, French astronomer Pierre Gassendi began making observations with a friend and colleague, Nicolas de Peiresc. By 1634 they had sufficient data to create their map, published in 1637 as *Phasium lunae icones* (see page 54).

THE MOON'S FEATURES EMERGE
As telescopes improved, astronomers were able to map the Moon in ever greater detail. The second half of the 20th century brought new breakthroughs. One was space flight: the ability to journey to or near the Moon and use some of the same mapping techniques we can use to map the Earth. The other was laser altimetry. This works by bouncing a low-intensity laser beam off the Moon's surface and measuring the time taken for the signal to return to Earth. The distance to the Moon's surface is calculated, giving the elevation at different points. Maps made in this way are built up by computers (see pages 68–9) and falsely coloured to show the range of altitudes.

Below: *Far from being featureless, the Moon has turned out to have a surface pitted with craters and dotted with mountains. This photo taken from Apollo 11 shows Crater Daedalus on the far side of the Moon.*

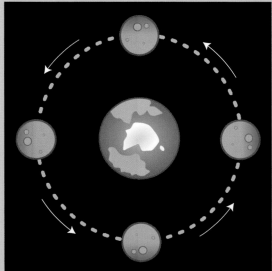

Until the late 20th century, all maps of the moon showed the same side. This is because the Moon is tidally locked to the Earth, so only one side is ever visible. The Moon takes approximately 27 days to rotate on its axis – the same amount of time it takes to orbit Earth.

In 1959, when spacecraft were finally able to travel behind the Moon and photograph it, humans saw the far side of the Moon for the first time.

The same side of the Moon always faces the Earth.

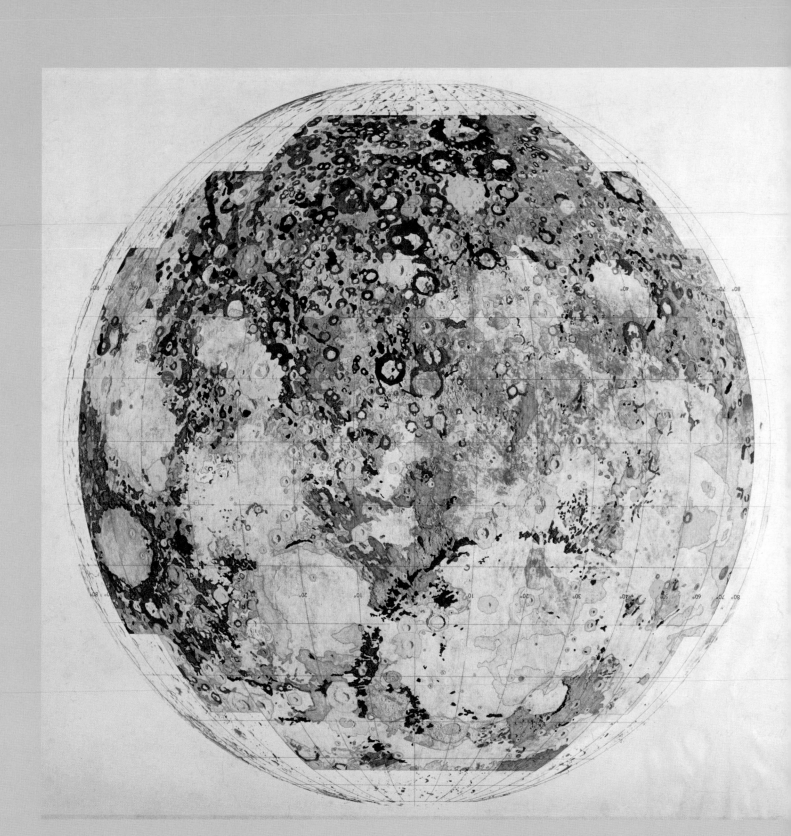

This geological map of the Moon was created in 1967 as part of NASA's preparation for the Moon landings. It was produced by combining data from photographs (many taken by Lunar Orbiter 4) and from observations by optical and radio telescopes, and measuring shadows to calculate elevations. The geology was calculated from observed differences in and layering of topographical forms, and in the amount of reflected sunlight (albedo), These both give clues to the underlying materials and methods of formation of features on the surface.

THOMAS HARRIOT, THE MOON, 1609–13

The English astronomer Thomas Harriot (1560–1621) was the first person ever to draw the Moon using a telescope, beginning several months before Galileo made his drawings in December 1609. Harriot's first sketch (right), made on 26 July 1609, shows an ill-defined patch of shadow in the position of Mare Crisium, together with the terminator – the boundary between the lit and shaded parts of the Moon. The sketch was made with a 'Dutch trunke' giving magnification x6.

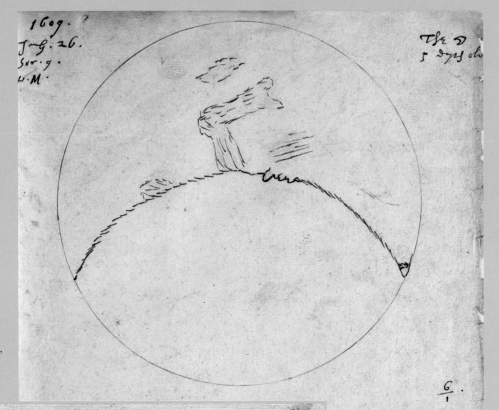

For his later Moon map (left), Harriot used a more powerful instrument – perhaps x20 or possibly even x50 magnification.

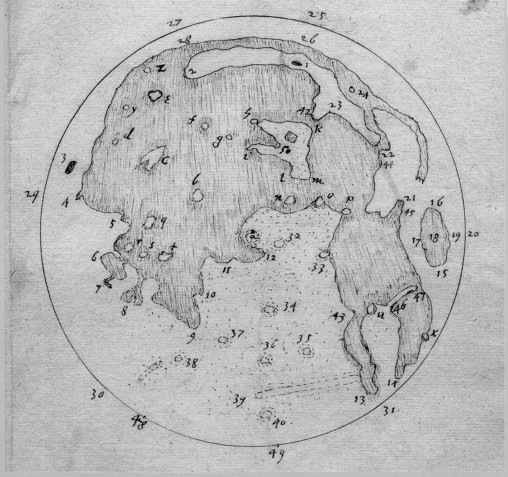

GALILEO'S DRAWINGS OF THE MOON, 1609

Galileo Galilei first heard of the existence of the telescope in 1609 in a letter from a friend, and set about making his own instrument. His was far better than the others in existence at the time. As soon as he turned it skywards, it revealed features never previously seen: the stars that make up the Milky Way, the moons of Jupiter, the rings of Saturn (which he first misinterpreted) and the uneven surface of the Moon. The latter was an immediate challenge to current orthodoxy, which held that the heavens were perfect and unchanging. Galileo wrote: 'It is full of inequalities, uneven, full of hollows and protuberances, just like the surface of the Earth itself, which is varied everywhere by lofty mountains and deep valleys.

'I have noticed that the small spots just mentioned have this common characteristic always and in every case: that they have the dark part towards the sun's position, and on the side away from the sun they have brighter boundaries, as if they were crowned with shining summits. Now we have an appearance quite similar on the Earth at sunrise, when we behold the valleys, not yet flooded with light, but the mountains surrounding them on the side opposite to the sun always ablaze with the splendour of its beams.'

Galileo's claim that the Moon had lofty mountains was provocative. In 1611, a year after he published his ideas in *Sidereus Nuncius* (*The Starry Messenger*), a group of Jesuit scientists examined the evidence and ruled against it, favouring the traditional account of a Moon with a perfectly smooth surface.

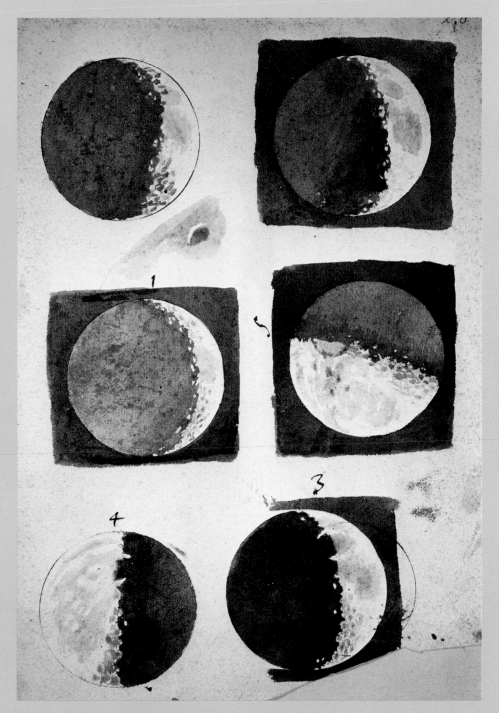

PIERRE GASSENDI & CLAUDE MELLAN, *PHASIUM LUNAE ICONES*, 1637

These three drawings of phases of the Moon were made by the French mathematician and astronomer Pierre Gassendi and engraved by Claude Mellan in 1637. Produced less than thirty years after the invention of the telescope, they already show a considerable increase in beauty, precision and attention to detail, including even the lines that radiate outwards from some of the impact craters. Gassendi was a committed believer in the Copernican model of the universe and a supporter of Galileo.

Above: First quarter, when half the waxing Moon is visible (about a week after a new Moon). The sunlight illuminating the Moon comes from the right.

Left: Full Moon, halfway through the cycle of the Moon's phases. The Moon is fully illuminated by the Sun.

Last quarter, when half the waning Moon is illuminated. Again, sunlight comes from the right.

MICHAEL VAN LANGREN, NAMING PARTS OF THE MOON, 1645

In 1645, Dutch astronomer Michael van Langren produced the first true map of the Moon, introducing his own conventions for nomenclature. He named the major features after Spanish royalty and Catholic saints, and the minor craters after astronomers, mathematicians and other scholars. Few of his names have endured as they were only of local interest, basically honouring people famous in Spain. Through mapping the Moon he aimed to provide a means of measuring longitude on Earth. He intended to produce 30 different detailed maps covering all the Moon's phases, which would allow determination of longitude on any day of the year. However, van Langren's plan was never realized. His was the best lunar map to date, but it was superseded just two years later.

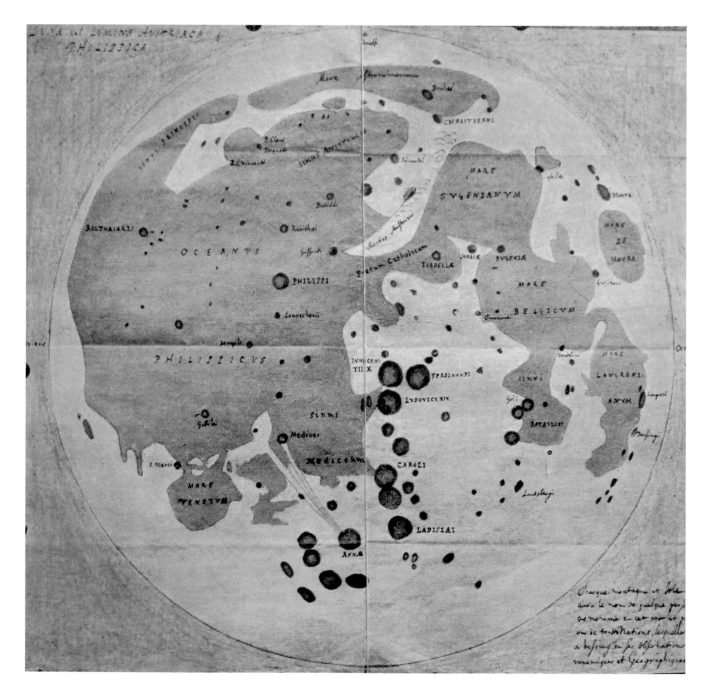

JOHANNES HEVELIUS, *SELENOGRAPHIA*, 1647

Johannes Hevelius was a Polish brewer who became adept at building telescopes. He observed the Moon over a period of four years, making detailed drawings and compiling them into *Selenographia,* the first atlas of the Moon. He repeated his observations again and again to perfect them, and even calculated the height of mountains on the Moon by measuring their shadows.

Hevelius's atlas included three large maps of the full Moon. One showed it as he saw it through his telescope; another followed the conventions of terrestrial cartography; the last was a composite map of all lunar features. This last established the tradition of showing a planetary surface with a single source of illumination that cast no features into shadow, impossible in any single view of the Moon in actuality. His were the most accurate representations of the Moon that had been drawn at the time and remained authoritative for 100 years.

Hevelius gave Greek and Latin names to the features he saw, including among them mountains (*mons*) and seas (*mare*). Dips he could see with the naked eye he designated *mare* and those he could only see through the telescope he designated craters. Although he named 268 features, only ten of his names are still in use. In a wonderful example of serendipity, he named the edge of the Sea of Tranquility 'Apollonia', and it was in this region that the Apollo missions landed more than 400 years later.

The double outline of the Moon in this and many later maps depicts the Moon's libration, the slight wobble which means that not exactly the same portion is visible all the time. The areas shown within the dotted line are sometimes visible, sometimes not, and account for 59 per cent of the Moon's surface. Libration was first described by Galileo in the 1630s.

FRANCESCO GRIMALDI AND GIOVANNI RICCIOLI, 1651

Jesuit astronomer Francesco Grimaldi worked closely with Giovanni Riccioli. His map of the Moon, published in Riccioli's *Almagestum Novum* in 1651, is based on earlier maps by van Langren and Hevelius.

   Riccioli divided the Moon into eight zones and gave the large features – the seas and plains – descriptive names such as 'Tranquility' and 'Serenity'. He followed van Langren in naming the craters after scholars, especially astronomers, and a few after saints with a connection to astronomy. Although Riccioli could not openly endorse the Copernican model of the cosmos that was opposed by the Church, he placed craters named after himself and Grimaldi alongside those named for Copernicus, which some historians take as tacit indication of support. Many of the names assigned by Grimaldi and Riccioli are still used.

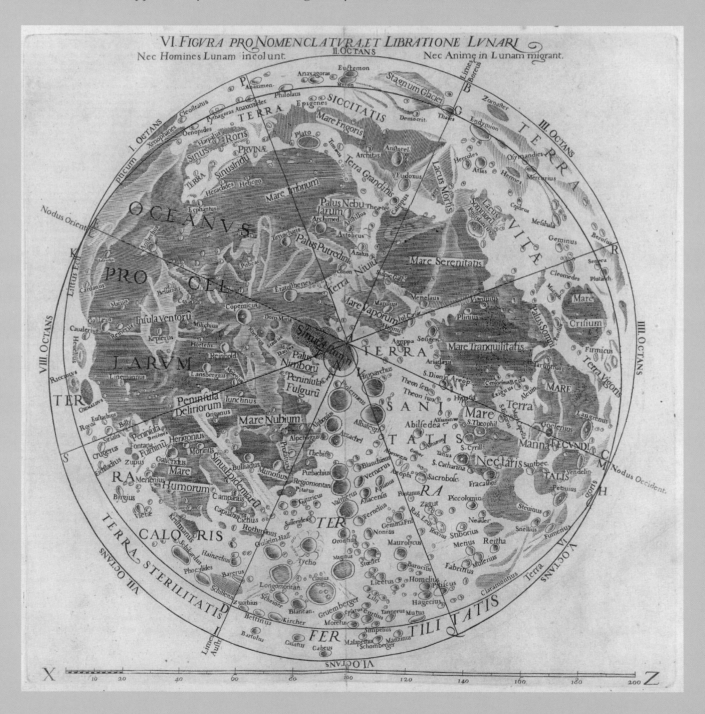

GIOVANNI CASSINI, MOON MAIDEN, 1679

Giovanni Cassini was an Italian astronomer and engineer. Working in collaboration with two artists, Sébastien Leclerc and Jean Patigny, he produced a series of detailed views of the Moon. Their collection of around 60 images formed a Moon atlas. In 1664, Cassini had begun working with a set of exceptionally fine new telescopes made for him by the expert lens-maker Giuseppe Campani in Rome. When Cassini moved to France to become head of the Paris Observatory, he took at least one of his telescopes with him. He was also famous for beginning the great project to create a topographic map of France, which would eventually be completed by his grandson more than 100 years later. He was able to do this after making the first successful measurements of longitude using the method outlined by Galileo; Cassini used his own tables of the moons of Jupiter as the basis for his system.

Cassini's finest charts of the Moon, such as the one above, published in 1679, remained the most detailed and accurate of their kind until the dawn of photography. This map is famous for details that are visible only in close-up, such as the 'Moon Maiden' in the area at the top left. A detail is shown on the left.

TOBIAS MAYER, 1748

Tobias Mayer was a German astronomer, mathematician and map-maker who used his combination of skills to improve the cartographic systems then in use. This chart of the Moon, published in 1748 in *Opera Inedita*, surpassed any previously made and remained the best available for 50 years. Mayer used a coordinate system and measured the positions of the craters precisely with a micrometer for the first time, achieving accuracy of one minute of latitude and longitude.

Mayer produced tables of the irregularities (perturbations) in the movement of the Moon, and studied the Moon's libration extensively. His tables and his own chart of the Moon refined the measurement of longitude at sea to an accuracy of half a degree. Although he died in 1762, before his tables were put to use, the Board of Longitude sent his widow £3,000 – a significant token of appreciation at the time.

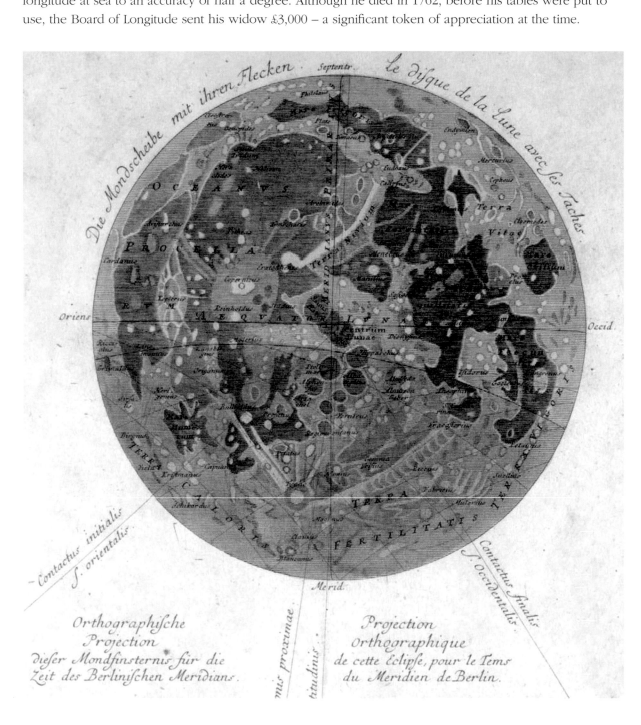

JOHANN HEINRICH MÄDLER AND WILHELM BEER, 1837

Two German astronomers, Johann Heinrich Mädler and Wilhelm Beer, worked together to map the Moon with a great degree of accuracy at an observatory they had funded and built themselves in Berlin (where Beer was a wealthy banker). They created the first detailed, exact map of the Moon, *Mappa Selenographica*, published in four volumes in 1834–6, and produced the map below, with a full description, in *Der Mond* the following year.

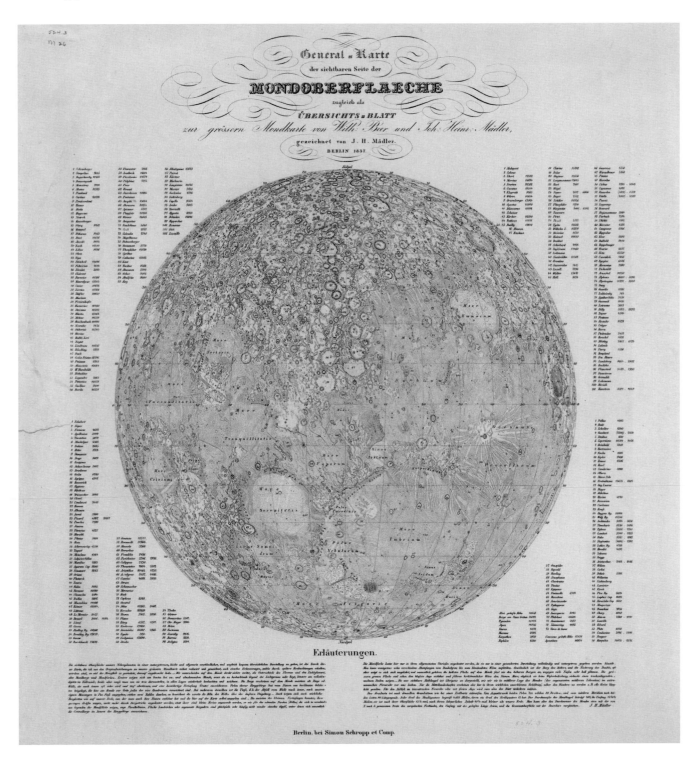

J.W. DRAPER, MOON PHOTO, 1850

The very first photograph of the Moon was taken in 1827 in France by Joseph Niépce. The following decade, his primitive process was replaced by one developed by another Frenchman, Louis Daguerre. In 1840, the Anglo-American scientist John William Draper took photographs of the Moon using a home-made telescope attached to a wooden box containing a photographic plate. He improved on Daguerre's chemical process, making portrait photography possible for the first time. Draper used a silvered glass telescope to produce the photographs. He is considered the first astrophotographer. Astrophotography now provides huge amounts of data for astronomy and forms the basis of most modern celestial maps.

Draper's very first image of the Moon, made in 1840, has probably been lost, but a photograph he took a few days later survives (left). It looks like a piece of abstract art. The image is vertically flipped, so the south of the Moon is at the top of the picture.

JOHN WHIPPLE, MOON PHOTO, 1857–60

John Whipple was a pioneering inventor and photographer and the first person to produce the chemicals needed for the daguerreotype process in America. He worked with the astronomer William Cranch Bond, director of the Harvard College Observatory, using the College's Great Refractor telescope to take the best photographs of the Moon of the time. Their work won the prize for technical excellence at the Great Exhibition in Crystal Palace, London, in 1851. Soon after, Whipple began to collaborate instead with James Black, with whom he produced this image of the Moon at some time between 1857 and 1860.

ÉTIENNE TROUVELOT, *MARE HUMORUM*, 1875

French artist and amateur astronomer Étienne Trouvelot made a series of astonishingly beautiful, detailed drawings from his astronomical observations, including this one of an area of the Moon, the Mare Humorum. Although lunar photography was gradually replacing drawing as the most accurate method of Moon mapping, Trouvelot's high-contrast, organic-looking pastel image is an evocative distillation of the Moon's mystery and beauty.

When the director of the Harvard Observatory became aware of Trouvelot's work, he invited him to join the staff. In 1875, when this image was produced, Trouvelot was working at the US Naval Observatory, where he had been invited to use the 26-inch refractor telescope for a year. He published 15 of his collection of 7,000 images in *The Trouvelot Astronomical Drawings*, 1881.

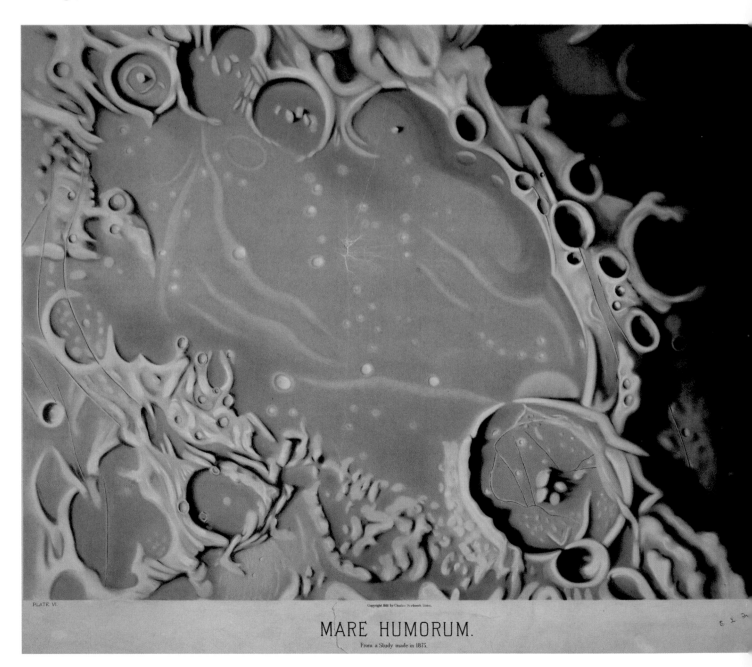

PLATE VI.   Copyright 1881 by Charles Scribner's Sons.

MARE HUMORUM.

From a Study made in 1875.

GEOLOGICAL MAP, USGS, 1961

In 1959, the first ever geological map of the Moon was begun by Arnold Mason
of the US Geological Survey with the aim of assessing the surface to find potential
landing sites. The Survey wanted to investigate the conditions that would face
vehicles landing on and moving over the Moon's surface, as well as astronauts
on foot, and even the possibility of building a Moon base. It based its work on
photographs taken at the Lick Observatory, San Jose, California. Those involved in
the mapping favoured the theory that craters are the results of impacts rather than
volcanic activity (their origins were still uncertain at the time). The first map was
published in 1960; a slightly amended version was produced the following year.

It was the first lunar map to show the chronological development of the Moon's
geological features. The small inset map is colour-coded to denote age. The areas
in brown were thought to be the oldest, predating the formation of the *maria*; the
maria are yellow; post-*maria* impact craters and features considered to be volcanic
are green. Black dots indicate items thought to be volcanic domes and black lines
tectonic faults – although, in fact, the Moon is not tectonically active. This map was
used by the lunar explorers in Arthur C. Clarke's *2001: A Space Odyssey*.

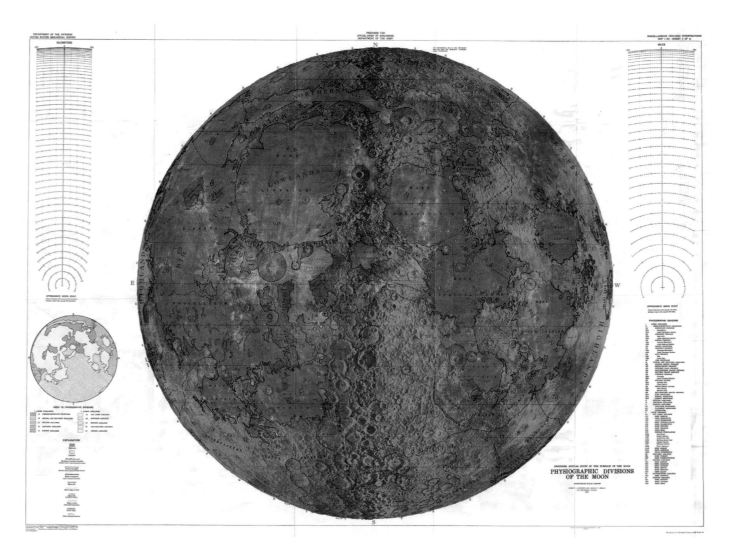

APOLLO 16, FAR SIDE OF THE MOON, 1972

The first photograph of the far side of the Moon was transmitted to Earth from the Soviet orbiter
Luna 3 on 26 October 1959. The lack of large features was an immediate surprise and puzzle to
astronomers. It has far fewer *maria* (lunar seas) – they cover only 1 per cent of the surface as opposed
to over 30 per cent of the Moon's near side. Instead, the far side is densely cratered.

   The first people to see the far side of the Moon other than in photographs were the crew of
Apollo 8 in 1968. Astronaut William Anders described it: 'like a sand pile my kids have played in for
some time. It's all beat up, no definition, just a lot of bumps and holes.' This photograph of the far side
was taken from Apollo 16 in 1972, the penultimate manned mission to the Moon.

MATERIALS OF THE MOON, 1992

Modern telescopy and photography can go far beyond taking a magnified picture of the surface of a celestial body. By taking images using light of different wavelengths – and sometimes not using visible light at all, but other parts of the electromagnetic spectrum – it is possible to resolve or deduce details otherwise not visible. This composite image of the Moon in false colours was built up from 53 pictures taken by the imaging system of the Galileo spacecraft using three spectral filters. It shows the northern regions of the Moon, with the part visible from Earth on the left. The colours correspond to the composition of the Moon: pink areas are highlands where igneous rock is common; blue to orange indicate hardened volcanic lava flows; mineral-rich soil is light blue and associated with recent impacts. The dark blue Mare Tranquillitatis contains more titanium than the green and blue areas seen above right. Blue rays extend outwards from the youngest craters.

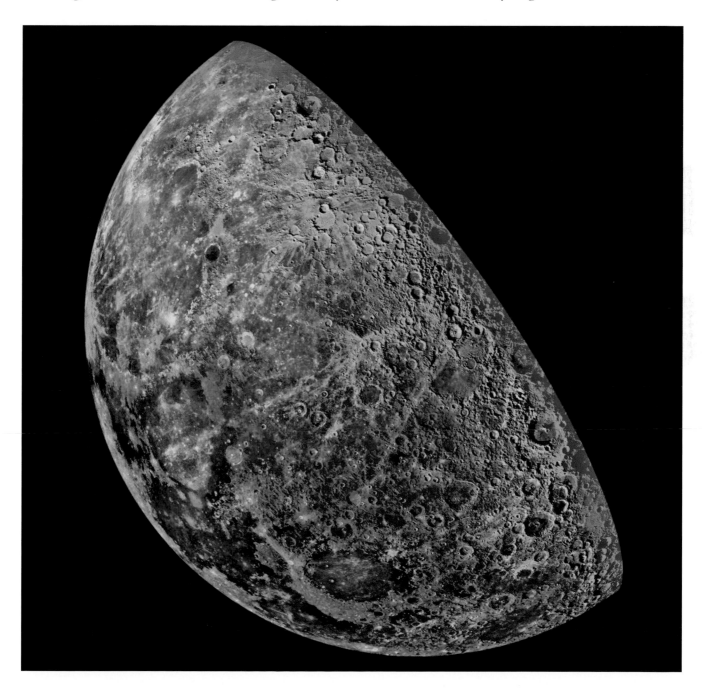

TOPOGRAPHY OF THE MOON, NASA, 2011

In 2011, NASA's Lunar Reconnaissance Orbiter science team released the highest resolution near-global topographic map of the moon ever created. Topographical maps of the Moon are colour-coded to show altitude. In these images, the lowest lying regions are blue, the highest are red. As the Moon has no sea level from which to measure altitude, the mean radius (1,737km/1,079 miles) is taken to be zero altitude. The altitude is determined using laser altimetry (see page 50).

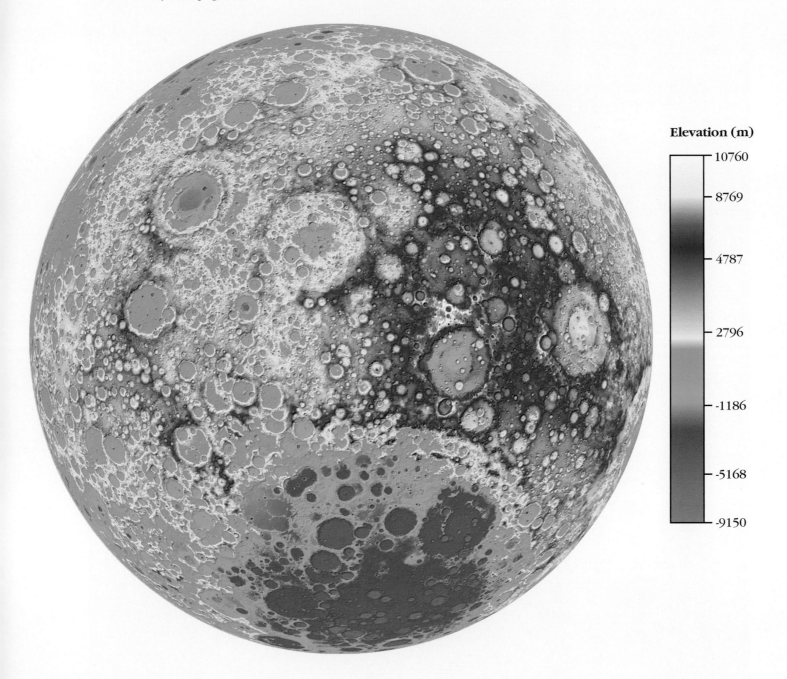

Elevation (m)

- 10760
- 8769
- 4787
- 2796
- -1186
- -5168
- -9150

GRAVITY MAP OF THE MOON, NASA, 2013

Gravity is not the same all over a rocky planet or moon – the lumps and bumps inside the celestial body and on its surface produce considerable variation. These differences have an impact on spacecraft flying around the Moon. In 2013, the Gravity Recovery and Interior Laboratory (GRAIL) mission mapped the gravity of the Moon. In the image below, the mean gravity, the value that would prevail everywhere if the Moon were entirely smooth and even, is shown in yellow. Red areas denote higher gravity and purple areas the lowest gravity. The area shown is on the far side of the Moon, with the impact feature Mare Moscoviense near the centre.

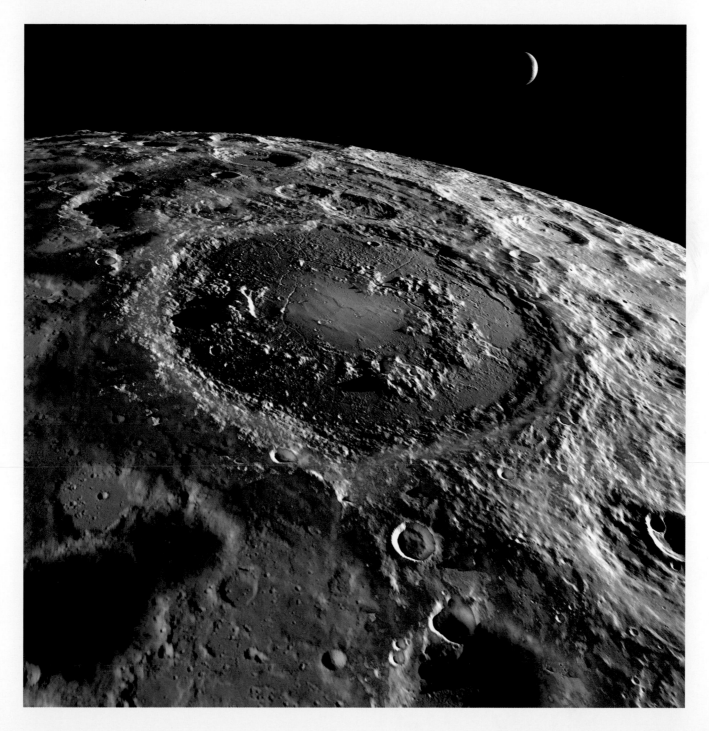

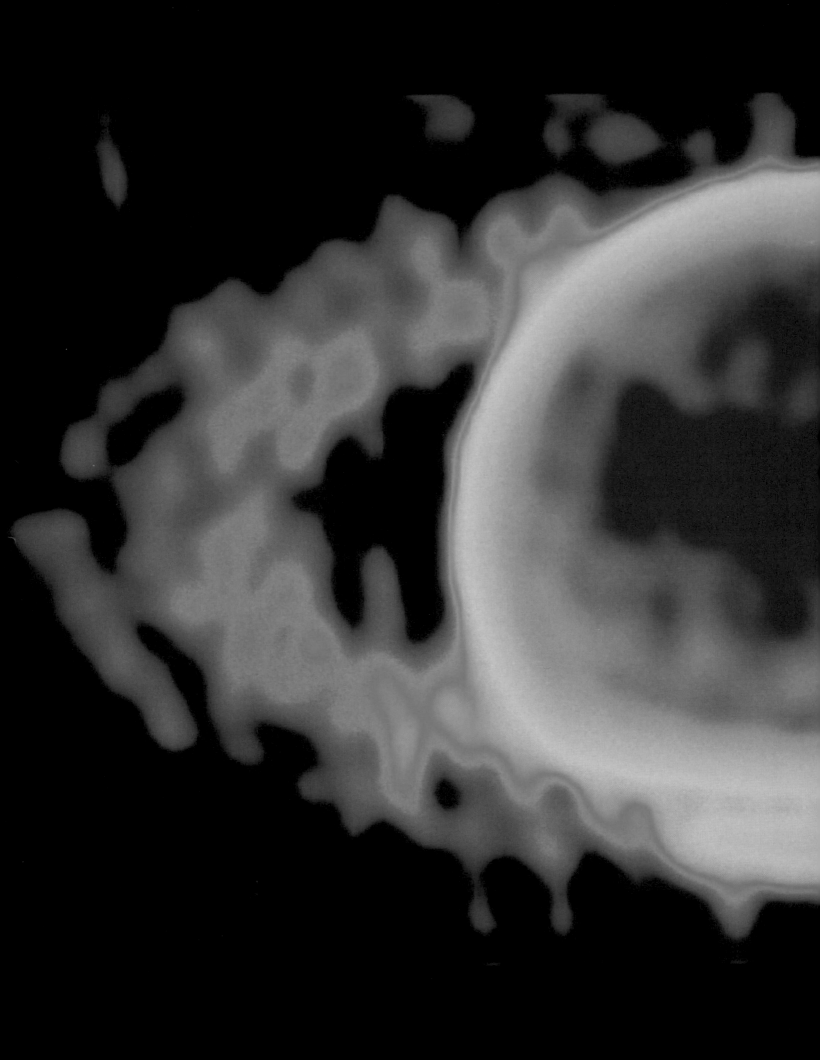

FROM POINTS TO PLANETS

OUR CELESTIAL BACKYARD

THE INVENTION OF THE TELESCOPE NOT ONLY opened up the Moon, but also revealed planets as worlds. Astronomers had already realized that there was a difference between the planets and the stars, but it had not previously been possible to tell just how different they are.

This false-colour radio map of Saturn was made using data from the Very Large Array telescope (VLA) in New Mexico, USA. The hottest part of Saturn appears red. The planet is tilted towards us, so that its rings cross the southern part as we look at it.

WANDERING STARS

To the naked eye, the planets look much the same as the stars. The only difference immediately apparent is that while the stars twinkle, the planets glow with a steady light. More importantly, and a feature our ancestors noticed and tracked, is that the planets move around the sky relative to the background of 'fixed' stars. The fixed stars move only en masse, the whole fabric of the sky apparently rotating around the celestial poles. The ancients called the planets 'wandering stars' – the word 'planet' comes from the Greek for 'wanderers' (πλανῆται, planētai) – but they had no way of knowing what they truly were.

Through the telescope, the planets emerged out of the darkness first as discs and later as the huge masses of rock, ice and gas we now know. The first telescopes revealed only very general surface features, and some of the rings and moons of the planets. As telescopes improved more features appeared, and it became possible to map the surface of the rocky planets. The gas giants have few stable features so could not be mapped in the same way. Telescopes revealed new planets, too. Only five (besides Earth) are visible to the naked eye and have been known since prehistoric times. Uranus was discovered in 1783, Neptune in 1846 and Pluto (briefly considered a true planet) in 1930.

This illustration from Physique Populaire *by Emile Desbeaux, 1891, focuses on comparing the sizes of the outer gas and icy planets, with Earth shown for comparison.*

Opposite: *This monstrous 40ft (12m) telescope belonged to William Herschel, who discovered Uranus in 1783. He built the telescope after he had discovered the planet.*

TOOLS FOR MAPPING

The earliest maps of the planets, like the early maps of the Moon, were low resolution, sketchy with scant detail. As telescopes improved, maps became more detailed until eventually photography extended the repertoire of astronomers and cartographers.

The greatest boon for the study of the planets, though, has been space travel. The ability to send probes with telescopes, cameras and scientific instruments into orbit around the planets, and even to land on some of them, has opened up the solar system to far more detailed investigation and mapping than ever before. We can now measure the composition, temperature and altitude of different regions of a planet.

NASA's Cassini spacecraft photographed plunging through a plume of liquid water and hydrogen erupting from the surface of Enceladus, one of Saturn's moons, in 2015. Enceladus is considered one of the more promising prospects for possibly hosting life in the solar system beyond Earth.

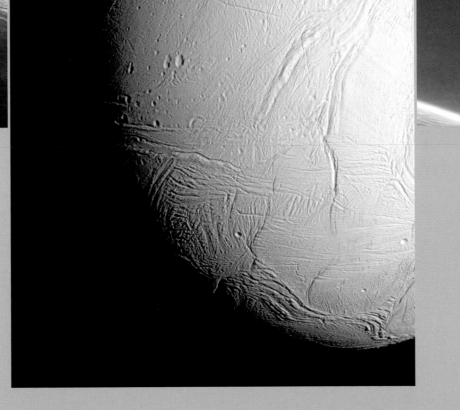

The surface of Enceladus is frozen, but is thought to cover an ocean of liquid water. The surface is marked by ridges, cracks and craters, the scars of tectonic activity and bombardment.

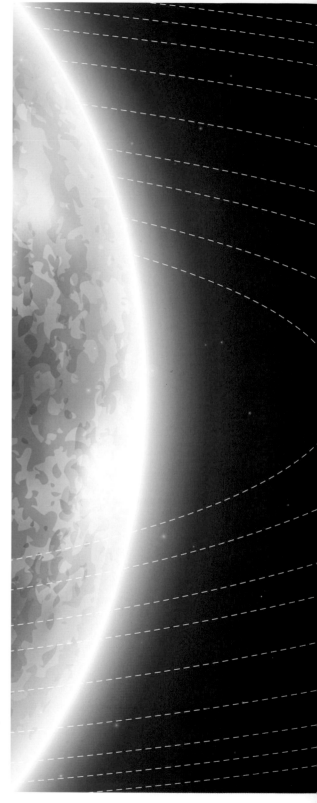

MEASURING LIGHT, AND OTHER THINGS . . .

An important means of gathering information about a planet is spectroscopy (see page 80), first used in the 19th century to identify elements by the light they emit or absorb. This involves measuring the wavelengths of the electromagnetic radiation (including visible light, radiowaves, infrared and ultraviolet) which reaches us from the planets.

The planets don't produce light, they reflect it from the Sun. But they don't reflect all the light (or other electromagnetic radiation) that falls on them. Some is absorbed by the gases, liquids and minerals which make up the planet. From examining the patterns of reflected radiation, astronomers can work out which bits have been absorbed. By comparing the bits that have been absorbed with the known absorption spectra of different materials, they can work out the composition of planets, either as a whole or region by region.

Similar techniques are used to determine the temperatures of planets and the amount of water present. Colours help to distinguish between regions of different composition or temperature.

Below: This false-colour image of the dwarf planet Pluto was produced by NASA from data gathered by the New Horizons mission in 2015. The central pink area is the Sputnik Planitia glacier.

The eight known planets of the solar system and the dwarf planet, Pluto. In sequence outwards from the Sun they are: Mercury, Venus, Earth, Mars, Jupiter, Saturn, Uranus, Neptune and Pluto. The Moon is shown with Earth, but the moons of other planets are omitted. In the following pages, we will deal with the planets in order of their proximity to the Sun, beginning with Mercury.

EUGÈNE ANTONIADI, *LA PLANÈTE MERCURE*, 1934

Mercury is a difficult planet to observe and yielded up few secrets until the telescope had developed considerably. In 1639, Italian astronomer Giovanni Zupus discovered that Mercury has phases, but he could not discern its surface. Giovanni Schiaparelli made the first attempt to record the surface features of the planet in 1889 and provided a coordinate system for the planet at the same time.

The first map of the surface of Mercury was drawn by Eugène Michel Antoniadi based on observations made in 1924, 1927, 1928 and 1929. He used the 83-cm Meudon telescope of the Paris Observatory – the same telescope he used to disprove the Martian canals theory (see page 91). Antoniadi based his map on the incorrect assumption that Mercury has one side permanently facing the Sun. In fact, Mercury rotates slowly, with a 'day' that is 58 Earth-days long, so his map is inaccurate.

The names Antoniadi assigned to the features he saw formed the basis of later naming conventions. In 1973, a Task Group for Mercury Nomenclature was set up to handle the naming of all new features. The rules are: large craters are named after authors, artists, and musicians; valleys are named after radio observatories; scarps are named after ships involved in exploration and scientific research; plains are named for 'Mercury' in various languages or after gods with equivalent roles in different cultures; and valleys are named after cities of antiquity.

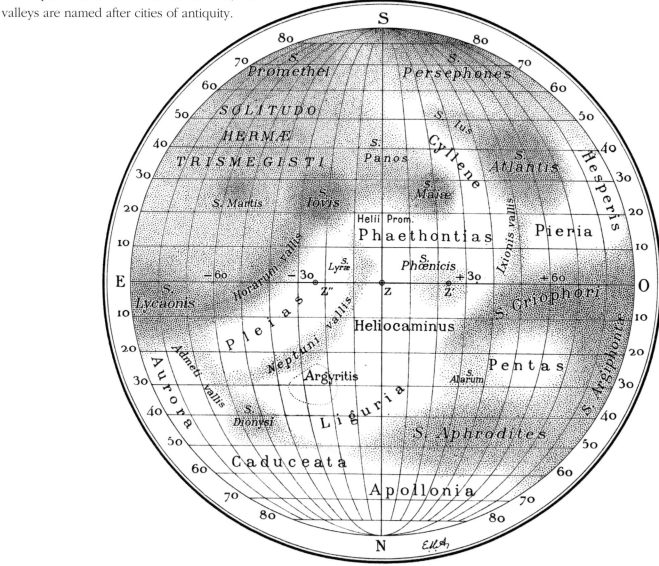

MARINER 10, MERCURY, 1974

This image of Mercury was produced by reprocessing data collected by the NASA Mariner 10 mission to Mercury in 1974. (The pale band represents an area for which there was no data.) Mariner photographed 45 per cent of the surface of the planet and the images were compiled into a partial map.

NASA, COMPOSITION OF MERCURY, 2012

This image was created by NASA's Mercury Atmospheric and Surface
Composition Spectrometer (MASCS). Consisting of two instruments that work with
electromagnetic radiation in wavelengths from ultraviolet to infrared, including
all visible light, MASCS examines the light reflected by the thin atmosphere and
the surface of Mercury. Each thin line shows the data for a single pass over the
planet, giving data for the area directly below the craft, so more densely coloured
regions were more frequently overflown. From the data collected, and the known
spectroscopic signature of the chemical elements, it's possible to work out the
concentration of different elements all over the planet.

   In this map, the wavelengths have been grouped and coloured so they can
be easily distinguished by eye. Eventually, data from MASCS will reveal much
valuable information about the composition of Mercury, its geological history and
the chemical interaction of the surface and the atmosphere.

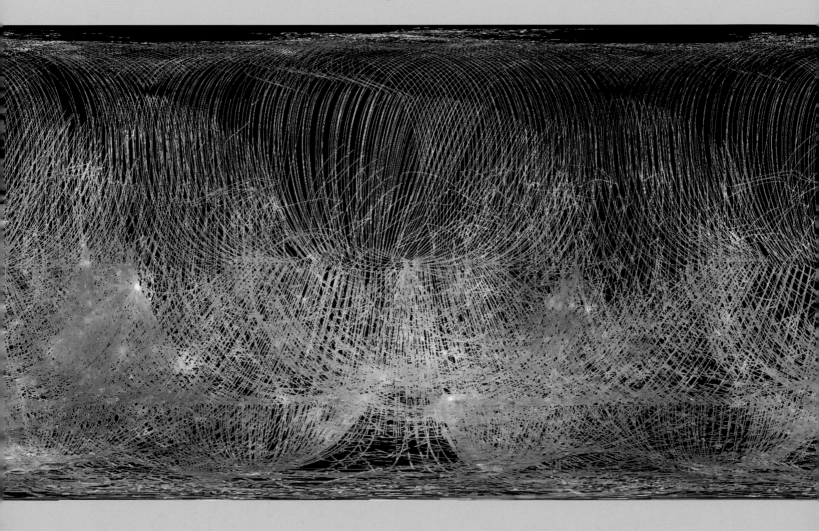

NASA MESSENGER, MAPPING MERCURY, 2016

Mercury was photographed and examined by NASA's Messenger probe in 2011–15. Messenger sent back 300,000 images, 10,000 of which were used to create a detailed mosaic map of the planet's surface. This enhanced colour image shows the elevation of the surface. As the planet has no oceans, elevation can't be measured from sea level and is instead specified relative to the average radius. Elevations range from the lowest point, 5.38km (3¼ miles) below the average, to the highest point, 4.48km (2¾ miles) above the average. The surface is marked by volcanic craters, wrinkled rock that represents hardened lava flows and impact craters caused by bombardment from space.

The Caloris Basin (left) is Mercury's youngest impact basin and one of the largest in the solar system at around 1,550km (963 miles) in diameter. It was probably formed 3.8–3.9 billion years ago by impact with a body at least 100km (62 miles) across. In this colour-enhanced image, the orange areas represent places that have been flooded by volcanic lava. Blue areas probably represent the floor of the basin and are where craters have been created since the last volcanic flood.

FRANCESCO BIANCHINI, THE SURFACE OF VENUS, 1728

Italian philosopher and scientist Francesco Bianchini examined the surface of Venus in order to calculate the planet's rotational period. He needed this information for his work on calendar reform, aimed at calculating the astronomically correct date for Easter.

Bianchini believed he had identified light and dark areas which corresponded to oceans and continents and named them accordingly. In the 17th century, the Italian astronomer Francesco Fontana had observed Venus and drawn its phases and a moon he claimed to have found, though Venus has no moon. Other astronomers claimed to be able to identify mountains on Venus. Christiaan Huygens (see page 104) stated correctly that Venus is surrounded by a very dense atmosphere: even if there were landmasses, mountains and seas, they would not be visible through the atmosphere.

Bianchini presented his map of the surface of Venus as gores, which can be cut and assembled into a globe.

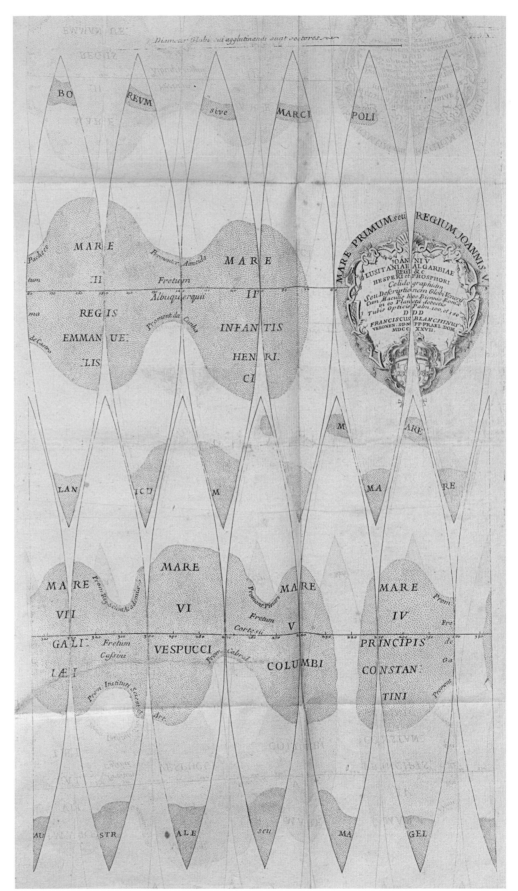

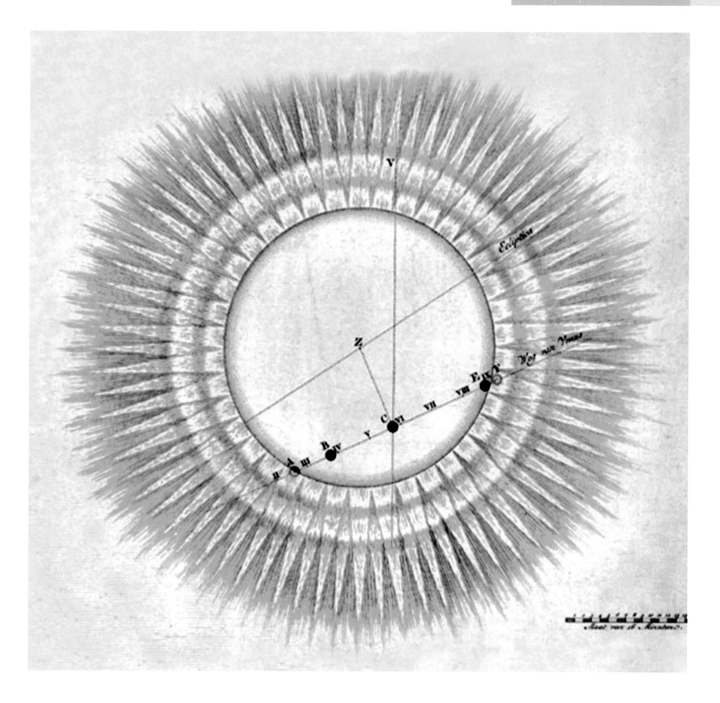

NICHOLAS YPEY, THE TRANSIT OF VENUS, 1761

This colour-enhanced drawing shows one of the rarest of planetary alignments – the transit of Venus across the disc of the Sun. During a transit, Venus can be seen from Earth as a small black disc.

Venus transits are historically of great scientific importance as they were used to calculate the distance from the Earth and other planets to the Sun. In 1761, astronomers used trigonometry together with the transit time of Venus observed from different places on Earth to work out the distance between Earth and Venus. Kepler had calculated the relative distances between all the planets and the Sun, and Venus was known to be 0.72 times farther from the Sun than Earth. Kepler's calculations made it possible to work out the distance between Earth and the Sun to around 152,887,680km (95,000,000 miles). This is quite close to the modern figure of 149,597,871km (92,955,807 miles).

USGS, VENUS TOPOGRAPHY, 1990s

Topographical data collected through ten years of radar investigation of Venus has been used to produce this map of the planet that can be folded into a globe. The Magellan mission of 1990–4 mapped 98 per cent of the planet's surface at a resolution of around 100m (109 yards). Maps were built up from radar image strips, covering areas 20km (13 miles) wide by 17,000km (10,563 miles) long (half the circumference of Venus), taken during the course of 4,225 orbits of the planet. The map is colour-coded to represent elevation. Gaps in the Magellan data were filled by data from the Soviet Venera missions.

Northern
hemisphere
of Venus

Magellan revealed that 85 per cent of the surface is covered by volcanic flows and the surface is around 500 million years old. Unlike Earth, where areas of high and low altitude tend to be concentrated in large areas (oceans, mountain ranges, plateaux), there is a jumbled mix on Venus. This is possibly because the high surface temperature of the planet enables volcanic lava to flow a long way before cooling and solidifying. The lack of water means that features are not eroded and re-formed as they are on Earth.

Southern
hemisphere
of Venus

RICHARD OF HALDINGHAM OR LAFFORD, MAPPA MUNDI, *c.*1300

For centuries, the Earth has been comprehensively mapped. The Mappa Mundi (world map) kept in Hereford Cathedral, England, was made around 1300 and shows the territories known at the time. Like other medieval world maps, it is a spiritual document as much as a cartographic one. It shows the locations of towns and rivers, but also shows real and mythical beasts, and different supposed races of humans, all annotated with information about them. East is at the top, and the holy city of Jerusalem is central. The map is drawn on a single piece of calfskin vellum. Maps of Earth are unique in being able to show human-made constructions and the distribution of living creatures. Maps of other planets can only show topographical features.

APOLLO 17, 'BLUE MARBLE', 1972

This iconic composite image of Earth from space (right) was taken from Apollo 17 and shows the Middle East, Africa, Madagascar and the south polar ice cap. The first picture of Earth from space was taken in 1946 from a V-2 rocket, but is almost unrecognizably grainy. Better pictures followed in 1947.

The first photograph to confirm Anaximander's assertion made 2,500 years earlier that Earth does, in fact, hang unsupported in space was taken in 1966 from NASA's Lunar Orbiter 1. The image (below) was not a planned part of the mission, which was intended to find potential landing sites on the Moon. At the very end of the mission, the camera was turned towards Earth in an inspired last-minute decision.

JOHANN MÄDLER AND WILHELM BEER, MARS, 1840

Galileo was the first person known to look at Mars through a telescope, but he could not discern any surface features. After him, Giovanni Cassini, William Herschel, Robert Hooke and Christiaan Huygens all sketched the patterns of light and shade they could make out on the planet, but the first attempt to map Mars was made by German astronomers Johann Mädler and Wilhelm Beer. From 1831, they developed a coordinate system and put the geological features they had identified on to a grid. Their prime meridian (the line north to south, labelled 0 here) is still used.

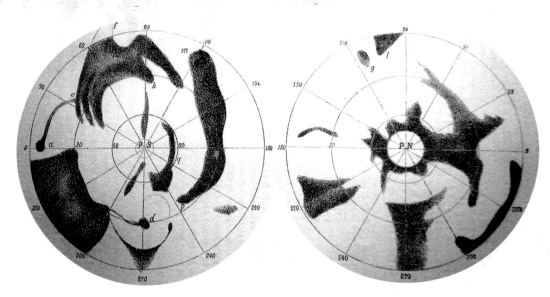

RICHARD PROCTOR, MARS, 1870

Later astronomers and artists continued to draw what they saw. The map below, which appeared in Richard Proctor's *Other Worlds Than Ours* (1870), is based on drawings by the Reverend W.R. Dawes. Proctor was the first to assign names to the areas which he took to be seas and continents, with ice caps at each pole.

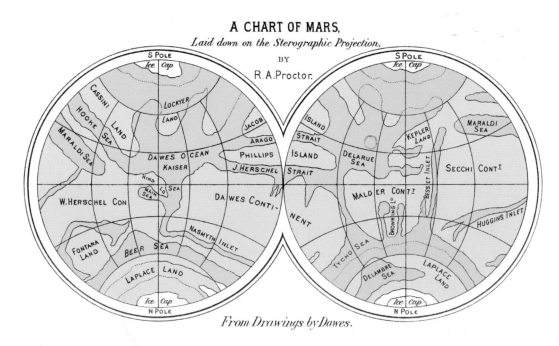

A CHART OF MARS,
Laid down on the Sterographic Projection,
BY
R.A.Proctor.

From Drawings by Dawes.

GIOVANNI SCHIAPARELLI, *CANALI* ON MARS, 1878

In 1877, Italian astronomer Giovanni Schiaparelli began mapping and naming the features he had seen on Mars through his telescope. He identified dark and light areas which he supposed represented land and water. His conclusion set a hare running. He used the Italian word *canali* for a network of lines he thought were channels carrying water. When translated into English, instead of 'channels' (which can occur naturally), *canali* was rendered as canals, suggesting they had been built by Martians. The idea soon took on a life of its own, with suggestions that the Martians were building canals to direct water from the poles to parts of their planet that were becoming parched, drought threatening their existence. An American businessman, Percival Lowell, became so obsessed by the Martian canals that he built an observatory to view them. Needless to say, there are no canals on Mars. The lines – which were seen by many people – were later identified as an optical artefact, a product of the telescopes in use at the time. They disappeared when telescopes improved.

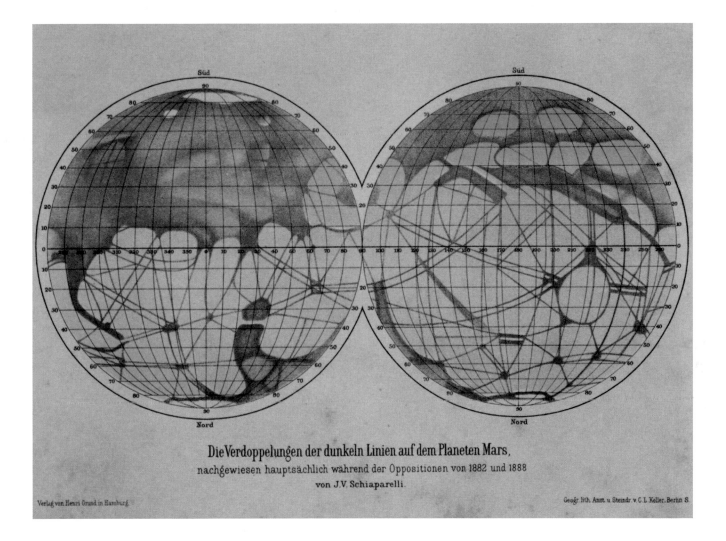

Die Verdoppelungen der dunkeln Linien auf dem Planeten Mars,
nachgewiesen hauptsächlich während der Oppositionen von 1882 und 1888
von J.V. Schiaparelli.

Verlag von Henri Grand in Hamburg.   Geogr. lith. Anst. u Steindr. v. C. L. Keller. Berlin S.

EUGÈNE ANTONIADI, MARS GLOBE, 1894

The Greek astronomer Eugène Antoniadi was originally a proponent of the idea of canals on Mars, and it was during this time that he made a globe based on maps of Mars drawn by Camille Flammarion in 1890. In 1909, Antoniadi came to the conclusion, now generally held as correct, that the straight lines described by Schiaparelli as *canali* were actually an optical artefact.

PERCIVAL LOWELL, CANALS ON MARS, 1908

Following Schiaparelli's report of *canali* on Mars, the American businessman and astronomy enthusiast Percival Lowell set out to prove the existence of the canals, which he thought were evidence of an advanced civilization capable of engineering work. In 1894, Mars was about to make a near approach to Earth, a mere 65 million km (41 million miles) distant. In readiness for this event, Lowell built an observatory at Flagstaff, Arizona, dedicated to studying the planet and – he hoped – revealing a Martian civilization. Needless to say, his ambition was not realized. But he did get to enjoy giving the theoretical canals mythological names, and Pluto was discovered at his observatory in 1930.

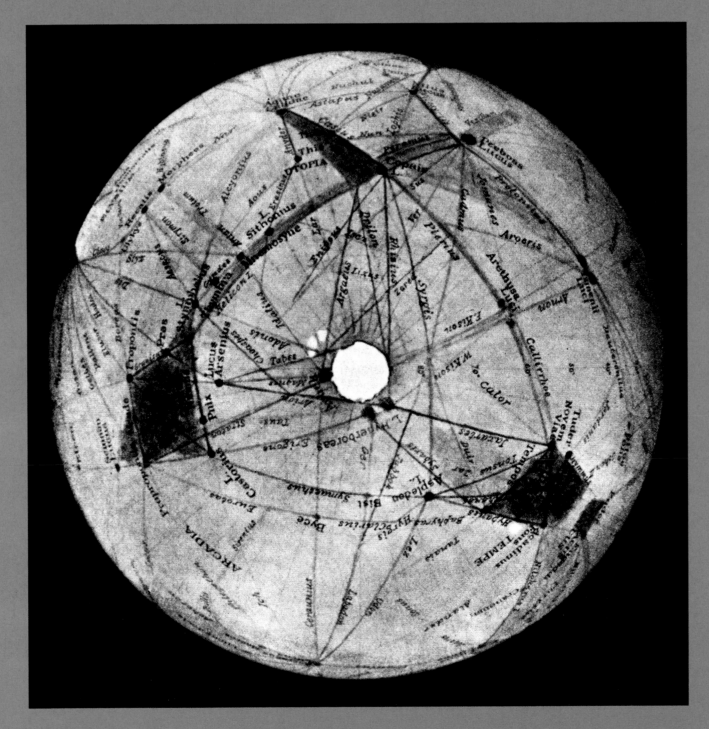

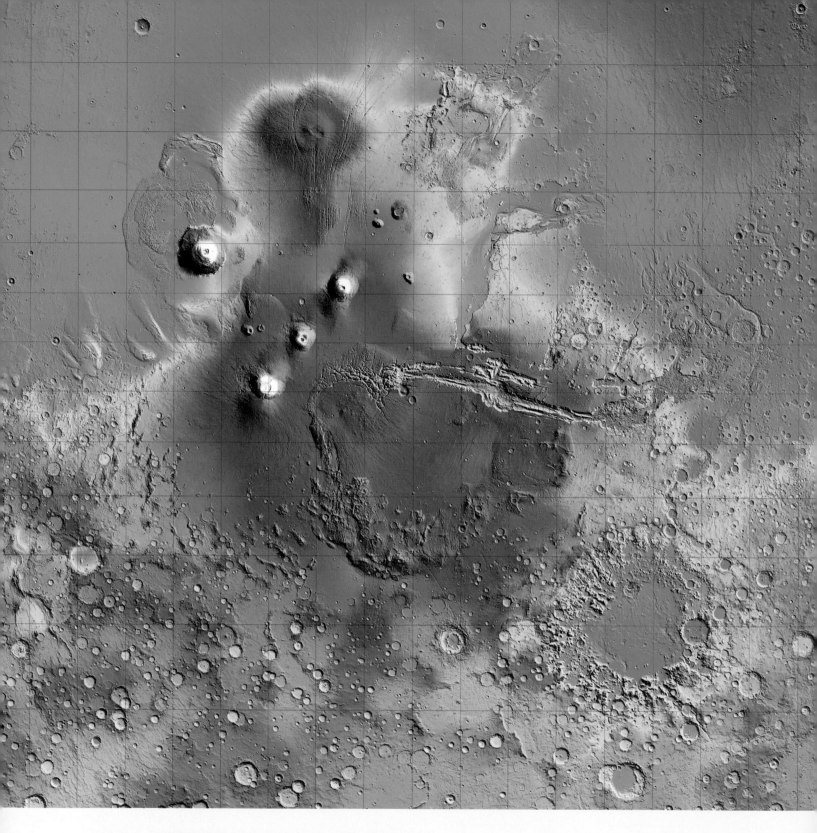

NASA, TOPOGRAPHY OF MARS, 2001

This topographical map has been constructed from data gathered by the Mars Orbiter Laser Altimeter (MOLA) on NASA's Mars Global Surveyor. Areas of lowest elevation are shown in blue, the higher land in red/brown and the peaks of volcanoes in white. The volcanoes of the Tharsis province on the left are taller than any mountains on Earth. The Valles Marineris to the right of the volcanoes is a canyon longer and deeper than the Grand Canyon in the USA. The deep-blue basin of the Hellas Planitia, more than 2,000km (1,242 miles) wide, was probably created by an asteroid crashing into the planet around 4 billion years ago. The north is predominantly smooth, with rough highlands in the south.

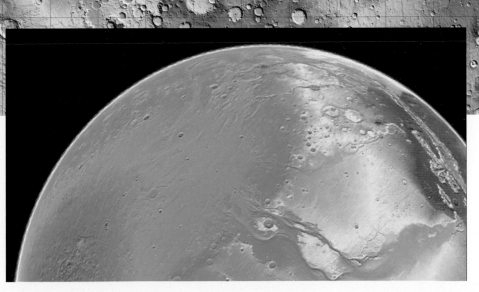

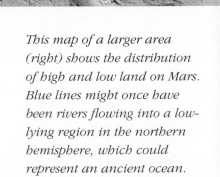

This map of a larger area (right) shows the distribution of high and low land on Mars. Blue lines might once have been rivers flowing into a low-lying region in the northern hemisphere, which could represent an ancient ocean.

USGS, MARS GEOLOGICAL MAP, 2014

Data from four Mars orbiter missions (Mars Global Surveyor, Mars Odyssey,
Mars Express and Mars Reconnaissance Orbiter) have been combined
to produce this geological map of Mars. It reveals the current geological
composition of the planet's surface and some of its history.
The extensive brown areas indicate surface
rock that is 4 billion years old.

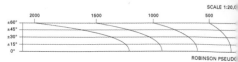

Right: This false-colour map of the topography on Mars shows volcanoes (with white peaks) on the left. These correspond to the volcanoes seen as reddish-brown circles on the geological map below.

30° 60° 90° 120° 150° 180°

REUM

Olympia Undae

OREALIS

UTOPIA

Lyot
Mensae

Protonilus Mensae

TERRA
Cassini

Arzachel

ISIDIS
PLANITIA

Nepenthes Planum

ELYSIUM PLANITIA

SYRTIS
MAJOR
PLANUM

Schiaparelli

SABAEA

Huygens

Gale

TYRRHENA
TERRA

HESPERIA
PLANUM

TERRA

Gusev

CIMMERIA

TERRA

HELLAS
PLANITIA

PROMETHEI
TERRA

Wallace

MALEA
PLANUM

Planum

TRALE

30° 60° 90° 120° 150° 180°

30°

0°

-30°

-60°

AT LAT ±38°

500 1000 1500 2000 KILOMETERS

±60°
±45°
±30°
±15°
0°

ION WITH POLE LINE

DONATO CRETI, JUPITER, 1711

Donato Creti's painting of astronomers observing Jupiter was one of a series of eight astronomical pictures commissioned from him by Luigi Marsili, Count of Bologna, and given to Pope Clement XI to persuade him of the value of funding an observatory. The gesture paid off, and the first public astronomical observatory was opened in Bologna. Creti's image of Jupiter shows the planet as it would have appeared through a telescope – its coloured bands could never have been seen with the naked eye. The three bright spots in line with it represent some of Jupiter's moons.

GALILEO GALILEI, THE MOONS OF JUPITER, 1613

Galileo first spotted and sketched the moons of Jupiter in 1610, but continued to track their movements, study and think about them. He published his full account in 1613, with representations of the configurations he had noted (see right). Depending on the positions of the moons relative to Jupiter (as one or more of them might be hidden behind the planet), Galileo saw two or three moons on some nights and occasionally even four. The largest of Jupiter's 67 known moons, these are known as the Galilean moons: Io, Europa, Ganymede and Callisto.

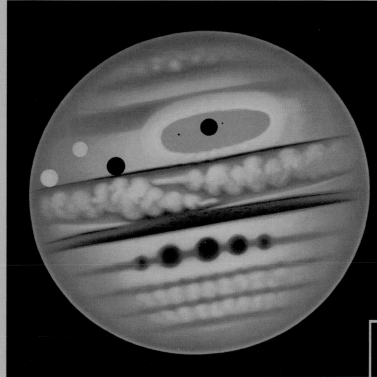

ÉTIENNE TROUVELOT, JUPITER AND ITS MOONS, 1880

Trouvelot's painting of Jupiter (above) shows its Great Red Spot, bands of cloud and moons. Although stylized, the main features of the planet are clearly visible, and the image is far clearer than photographs of the time. The black and white spots represent moons passing across the face of the planet. By contrast, the photo of Jupiter taken in 1879 (right) shows only the dark equatorial band and the Great Spot, both poorly resolved.

1879

DAMIAN PEACH, JUPITER'S GREAT RED SPOT, 1890 AND 2015

The most noticeable feature of Jupiter is the Great Red Spot, first recorded either by Robert Hooke in 1664 or Giovanni Cassini in 1665 (Hooke may have referred to a spot in the northern hemisphere). The spot is a giant storm twice the size of Earth, with winds whirling at 643km per hour (400mph). It was observed repeatedly until 1713, but then there is a gap in the record of 118 years until 1830, meaning that the spot we see now is not

necessarily the same as the one originally detected. Images show how the spot has changed between 1890 and 2015. Using software designed to measure features on Jupiter, amateur astronomer Damian Peach constructed the image on the left from photographs taken at the Lick Observatory in 1890. Then the spot was 40,000km (25,000 miles) across – about twice the size it is now. A new spot formed in 2000, when three smaller storms combined. It was initially white, but has now gained a reddish hue. Mapping and tracking the spots and bands on Jupiter helps us to understand the planet's weather system.

CASSINI, POLAR MAPS OF JUPITER, 2000

These two images show the whole of Jupiter. The one on the right shows the north pole to the equator and the one below shows the south pole to the equator. Cloud formations, vortices and bands of coloured gases form the thick outer layers of the gaseous planet. The Great Spot can be seen in the southern hemisphere as a bulge in the outer reddish-brown band of cloud.

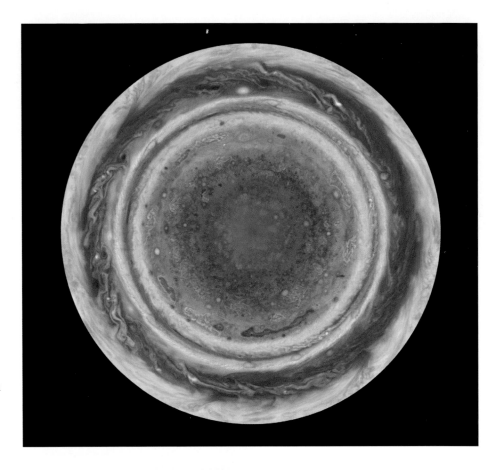

NASA, TRIPLE ECLIPSE OF JUPITER, 2004

This false-colour image of Jupiter taken by the Hubble Space Telescope in 2004 shows a triple eclipse by three of its moons. The three dark circles are the shadows of the moons, from left to right, Ganymede, Io and Callisto. Two moons are visible in the centre: Io is white and Ganymede is blue.

ESO, JUPITER IR, 2016

This image of Jupiter shows the planet mapped by its temperature. The coolest areas are dark red, the hottest are yellow and white. It was produced using an infrared imaging instrument on the European Southern Observatory's Very Large Telescope (VLT), by combining the best from a large collection of images and putting them together to form a complete heat map of the planet.

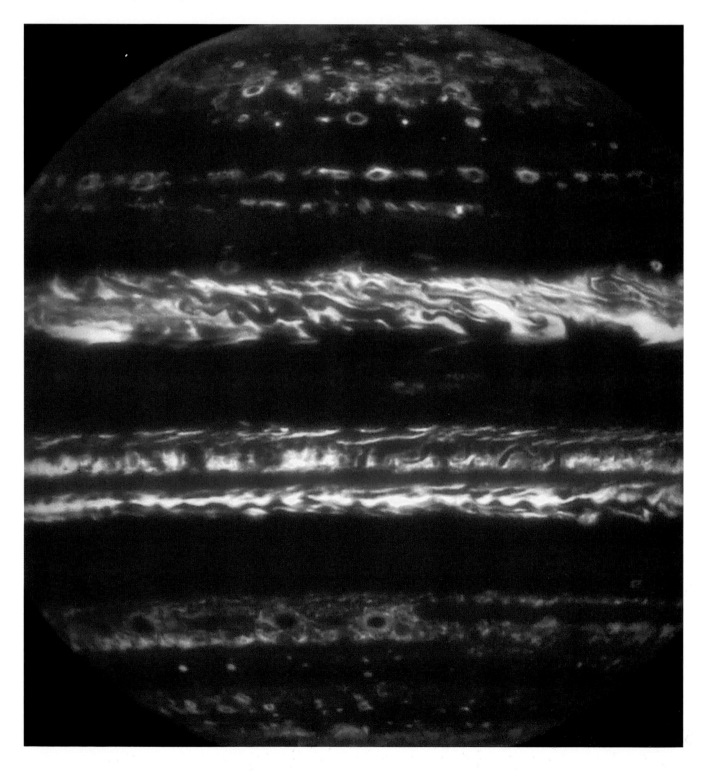

JUNO, SOUTH POLE OF JUPITER, 2017

NASA's Juno mission to Jupiter and its moons began in earnest in 2016 with the spacecraft's arrival at the planet. Juno is using instruments which can penetrate Jupiter's atmosphere to investigate its interior and map its strong electric and magnetic fields. This image shows storms swirling over the south pole of the planet. Juno has discovered a previously unknown band of ammonia rising from at least 320km (200 miles) down, and readings suggest there is no solid rocky core but perhaps a large 'fuzzy' one with no distinct boundary.

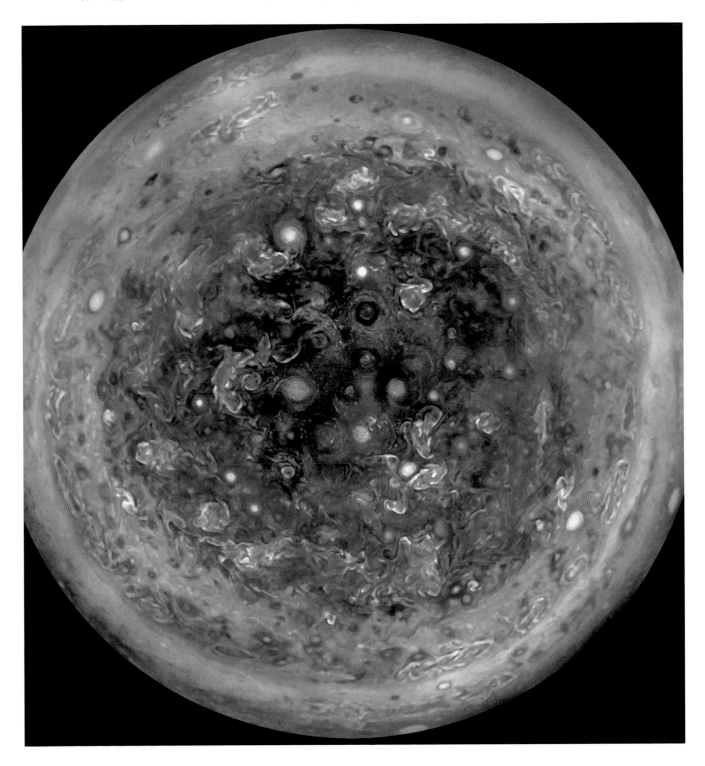

CHRISTIAAN HUYGENS, SATURN'S ORBIT, 1659

The appearance of Saturn through early telescopes presented a curious puzzle to astronomers. At first it appeared to have bulges, like ears, then these moved and vanished, before reappearing. Galileo reported in 1610 that: 'Saturn is not a single star, but is a composite of three, which almost touch each other, never change or move relative to each other, and are arranged in a row along the zodiac, the middle one being three times larger than the lateral ones, and they are situated in this form: oOo.'

He was wrong about them never moving, as became clear when he reported in 1612 that the 'ears' had disappeared. The question was solved by the Dutch astronomer Christiaan Huygens in 1659. In his *Systema Saturnium* he proposed that Saturn is surrounded by a thin, flat ring. By tracking the orbit of Saturn and its largest moon, Titan (which Huygens discovered), he revealed how the appearance of the planet changes according to its position in relation to Earth.

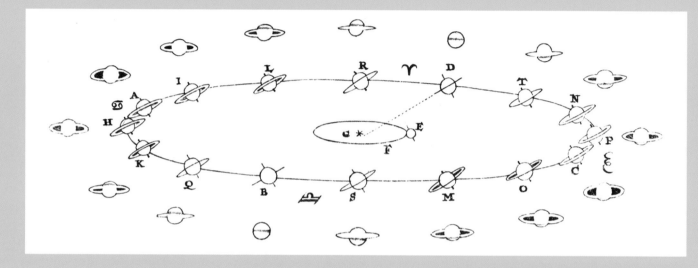

NASA, SATURN'S RINGS, 2004

This false-colour image of Saturn's rings was made from photographs taken by Voyager 2. It allows mapping of the rings to highlight differences in their composition and features. They are in fact coloured, though less vividly than in this image. The colours may be imparted by impurities in the ice making up the rings or may arise from damage to the crystalline structure of the ice. The rings are thought to be no more than 200m (220 yards) thick. The area covered by the image measures 68,000km (42,250 miles) top to bottom.

CASSINI, SATURN'S NORTH POLE, 2012

The north pole of Saturn is characterized by a bizarre hexagonal jet stream which is an enduring feature. At the very centre, above the pole, is a massive hurricane with an eye 50 times larger than that of a typical hurricane on Earth. Reddish ovals represent small vortices; a large white vortex below the pole is a hurricane 3,500km (2,175 miles) across. Some of the inner vortices spin clockwise, while the hexagon and large hurricane spin anticlockwise. The hexagon is twice as wide as Earth and its jet stream travels at 98 metres per second, or more than 350,000kph (217,500mph). This vortex was mapped by the Cassini probe.

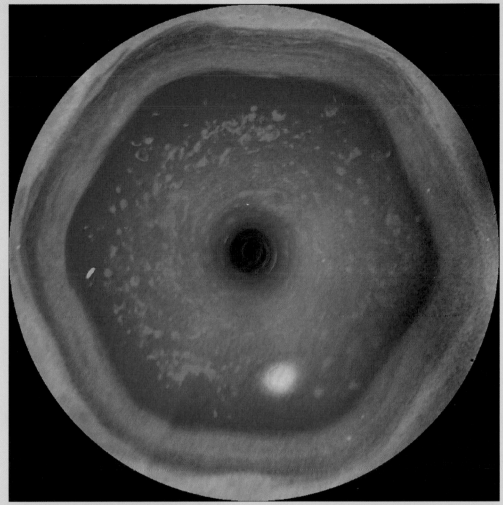

Saturn is a gas giant, so all its features are parts of its weather system, meaning that any map is accurate only transiently. Even so, while hurricanes on Earth last around a week at most, the hexagon has been whirling for decades and perhaps longer. It was first identified in 1981 by the Voyager mission.

NASA, SATURN, NORTHERN HEMISPHERE, 2016

This composite image taken by the Cassini-Huygens craft in 2016 shows the northern hemisphere of Saturn as it approaches midsummer. The year on Saturn is 30 Earth years long. Cassini has recorded substantial changes to the appearance of the planet during its observations spanning nearly half a Saturnian year. The photos used to make this image were taken from a distance of 3 million km (1.9 million miles).

NASA, TITAN, 2014

Saturn's biggest moon, Titan, is the second-largest moon in the solar system. It is the only body besides Earth known to have oceans of liquid on its surface, though in the case of Titan they are oceans of methane. The bright area near the top left is 'sunglint' caused by the Sun reflecting off the surface of the ocean at just the right angle to be caught by the camera of the Cassini-Huygens probe. Some hills and mountains on Titan have been named after characters and places in J.R.R. Tolkien's fiction, including Gandalf, Arwen, Bilbo Baggins and Mount Doom.

VOYAGER 2, URANUS, 1986

In 1781, William Herschel discovered Uranus, the first planet to be found using a telescope. It was identified as a planet in 1783. Mapping Uranus would be a dream job for the laziest of cartographers. Images taken by Voyager 2 in 1986 show it as a completely featureless pale-blue disc, an ice giant lacking the storms and clouds of the other gas giants.

But Uranus has not remained as entirely featureless as it first looked. Bands of cloud are sometimes visible, and the brightness of the polar areas alters. It appears that these changes in the atmosphere might be seasonal, but as detailed observation has not yet followed a full year on Uranus (84 Earth years), it is too early for conclusive findings. Pictures taken by the Hubble Space Telescope in 2006 reveal more cloud and faint rings, and Uranus seems to have become more like the other gas giants as its year progresses. There are 13 faint rings and 27 small moons. Uranus, the 'sideways planet', is unusual in having its axis effectively east–west rather than north–south – the only planet in the solar system to do so.

JAMES GLAISHER, DISCOVERY OF NEPTUNE, 1846

Neptune was the first planet to be predicted to exist before it was discovered. Both the French astronomer Urbain Le Verrier and the English astronomer John Couch Adams had predicted the location of an unknown planet based on perturbations in the orbit of Uranus. The planet was found by Johann Gottfried Galle at the Berlin Observatory on 23 September 1846. It was still unnamed when this drawing was made. Neptune's locations at its discovery and a week later are marked in the constellation of Aquarius – three squares from the left and two squares down. This map was published in *The Illustrated London News* alongside a letter from British meteorologist James Glaisher concerning the discovery.

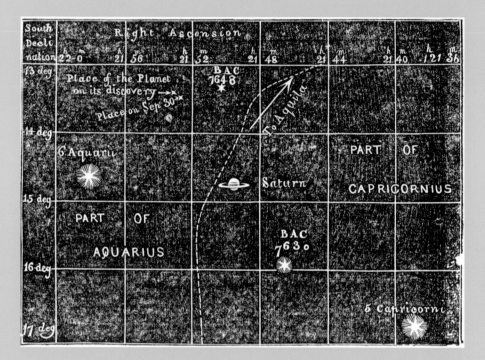

VOYAGER 2, NEPTUNE, SOUTHERN HEMISPHERE, 1989

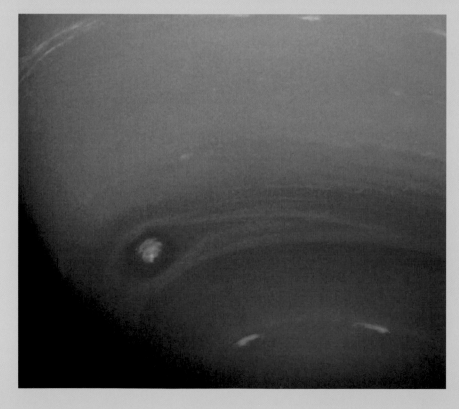

Like those of the other gas giants, Neptune's features are restricted to its atmosphere and, as such, are transient. Its atmosphere consists mostly of hydrogen and helium and is tempestuous on a grand scale. The spot on the left of the picture represents a vortex of whirling winds that is the size of Earth. Neptune has the most vicious winds in the solar system, blowing at up to 2,100kph (1,300mph) – nine times the speed of the most powerful winds recorded on Earth. The light patches are methane clouds that have precipitated out of the atmosphere, which is thought to be layered, with some of the visible methane clouds casting shadows onto different clouds 56km (35 miles) below them.

VOYAGER 2, TRITON, 1989

This image of Neptune's moon Triton is a mosaic of photos taken by Voyager 2 as it passed in 1989. Voyager is the only craft to have approached Neptune and its moons. The surface of Triton is covered with nitrogen snow. The temperature is -236 degrees Celsius, the coldest known surface temperature in the solar system, and much of its nitrogen-based atmosphere has frozen. The pinkish areas are the southern polar cap containing methane ice, some of which might have formed reddish compounds under the influence of sunlight. The band that extends around the equator is thought to be an area of more recently formed ice. Ice volcanoes and geysers are still active.

HUBBLE SPACE TELESCOPE, NEPTUNE, 1996

Images taken by the Hubble Space Telescope in 1996 in different wavelengths of light reveal the composition of Neptune's atmosphere. The main body of the atmosphere is blue, a shade produced in part by methane. White clouds are above this layer, and the highest clouds appear yellow-red. The powerful equatorial jet-stream is centred on the dark blue band just below the equator. The composition of the atmosphere further south must be different; the green belt shows an area where blue light is absorbed, but this has not yet been fully explained.

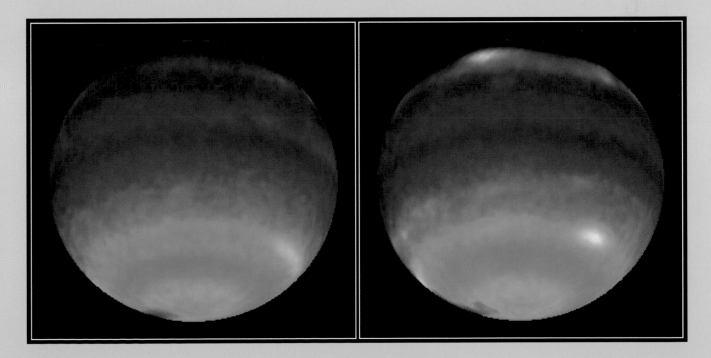

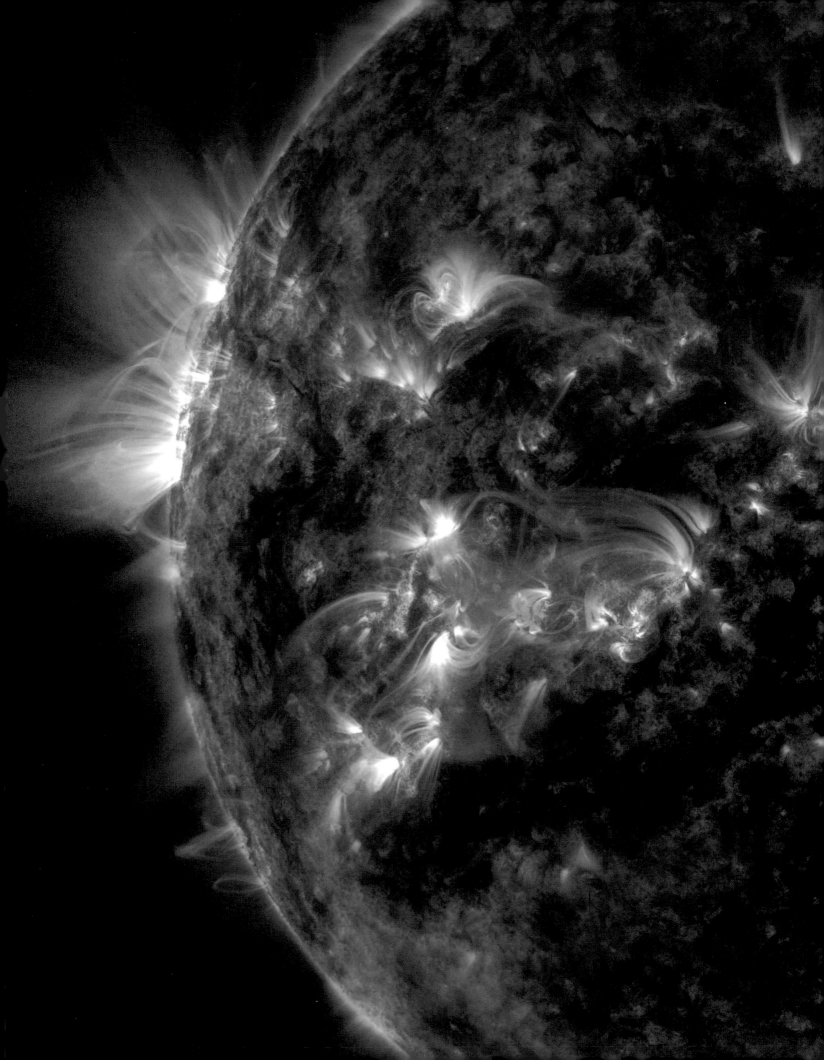

THE SUN IN ITS SYSTEM

SOL, THE NEAREST STAR

THE SUGGESTION THAT THE SUN MIGHT BE A star like any other recurred intermittently from the time of the Ancient Greeks, but was not popular in Christian Europe. It did not seem to fit with the position in the universe which God had appointed for humankind. But towards the end of the 16th century the model of an unchanging, divinely ordered, celestial universe centred on humanity started to become untenable.

Bright spots and arcs on the surface of the Sun indicate areas of activity, but they are transient. There is no stable map of the Sun, as its surface is constantly changing.

THE CHANGEABLE HEAVENS

The cosmic systems of Ptolemy, Copernicus, Tycho and others dealt theoretically with the relationships and hierarchy of the solar system, but did not deal with distances within it, the movement of comets or the nature of the Sun itself. With the further development of the Copernican system, and particularly Kepler's refinement of it in the early 17th century, that changed.

In the 1570s, two unusual celestial events upset the traditional view of the heavens as perfect and unchanging. At the start of the following century, in 1609, the telescope revealed the Moon's 'imperfection' and soon showed sunspots which seemed to be flaws in the face of the Sun. During the following centuries a scientific approach to the cosmos would gradually replace the traditional paradigm.

Tycho Brahe's comet of 1577. The comet is shown in front of the clouds, reflecting the contemporary view that comets were in Earth's atmosphere.

Copernicus published his model of the solar system in *De revolutionibus* in 1543. Less than 30 years later, the first of two disruptive astronomical events occurred. A brilliant new star appeared in 1572. It disappeared again after a few months, but by then it had already disrupted the Aristotelian ideal of an eternally fixed and perfect universe. The 'star' would be identified much later as a supernova, the catastrophic explosion of a star that has reached the end of its life. The next challenge came in the form of a comet, just five years later. The *Silk Atlas of Comets*, dating from 185BC, presents a taxonomy of comets, illustrating the different types observed.

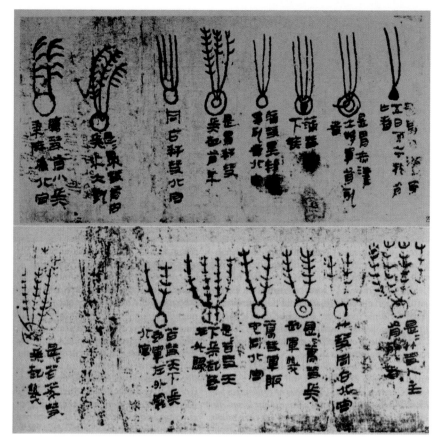

Above: The Silk Atlas of Comets, *created around 185BC, depicts the different types of comets recognized by Chinese astronomers.*

While Chinese astronomers had been attempting realistic depictions of comets for centuries, Europeans produced fanciful images such as this. The comet, seen in 1527 over Germany, is described as having the appearance of a bent arm holding a sword with three stars at its point.

Comets were generally believed to be meteorological phenomena, and to belong in the sub-lunar region. Aristotelian cosmology placed a firm dividing line at the sphere of the Moon; everything below the line was changeable and corrupt, and all above was perfect, unchanging, and capable of only circular movement. To fit this scheme, comets had to belong to the lower realm, so it was assumed that they occurred within Earth's atmosphere. The comet of 1577 directly challenged the Aristotelian model.

The comet of 1577, from the Turkish treatise Tarcuma-I Cifr al-Cami by Mohammed b. Kamaladdin, 16th century.

Tycho Brahe measured the distance to the comet using a method known as parallax. This uses the displacement against a background which occurs if an object is viewed from two different lines of sight. (You can experiment by holding a finger in front of your face and looking at it with one eye at a time – the finger appears to move from side to side.) Parallax revealed the comet to be four times farther from Earth than the Moon. In Aristotelian terms it belonged to the fixed, unchanging heavens, but, disturbingly, it represented a changing rather than a fixed element.

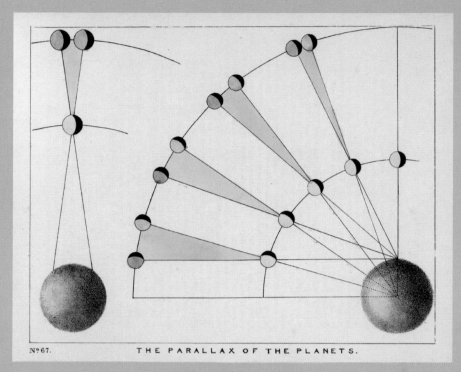

N.º 67.   THE PARALLAX OF THE PLANETS.

Above: A diagram showing how parallax works, published in 1849. The position of a planet relative to the Moon is measured from different positions on Earth. From the apparent difference in position, the distance to the planet can be calculated. The smaller the difference, the further away the planet. For this reason, the position of stars could not be calculated by parallax until recently as the difference was very small.

As soon as the telescope was put to use, sunspots became clearly visible as dark patches on the surface of the Sun. In fact, they had been observed as early as 800BC in China, and from 300BC in Europe. European observers had generally assumed that they were planetary transits. For the European astronomers of the 17th century, the phenomenon of sunspots appeared as a new discovery. They were another blow to the supposed perfection of the heavens.

Left: The earliest known drawing of a sunspot is in the Chronicle of John of Worcester, *written in 1128.*

LAMBERT DE SAINT-OMER, THE 'MUNDANE YEAR', *LIBER FLORIDUS*, 1121

This diagram from a 15th-century copy of Lambert de Saint-Omer's encyclopaedia *Liber floridus* shows the alignment of the Sun, Moon and planets in a straight line to explain the 'mundane year' as described by the Roman philosopher Macrobius in the 5th century AD. Modelled on the Ptolemaic system with the Earth at the centre, the mundane year had a duration of around 15,000 years and was the time taken for all the celestial bodies, including the fixed stars, to return to an original starting position. The calculation of the length of the mundane year given in *Liber floridus* is 16,416 years, which he seemed to consider close enough. Perhaps wishing to be economical with his diagrams, Lambert has included a depiction of five phases of the Moon, and an extra image of the Sun at the bottom showing how the Sun's light illuminates the Moon and produces its phases. The red text in the lower left explains that the Moon gains its light from the Sun.

JOACHINUS DE GIGANTIBUS, THE SUN, *ASTRONOMIA*, 1478

This image of the Sun (right), produced by Joachinus de Gigantibus, is taken from *Astronomia*, written by Christianus Prolianus and dating from 1478. It shows the comparative size of the Sun, and then (first row, left to right) Mars, the Moon, Venus, and (beneath) Earth and Mercury.

The illustration below shows Saturn and Jupiter. The sizes are nowhere near accurate: Mars is smaller than the Earth, the Moon is a good deal smaller than shown here, and Saturn and Jupiter, though large, do not approach the size of the Sun.

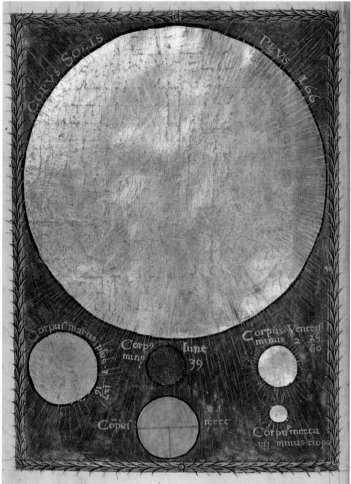

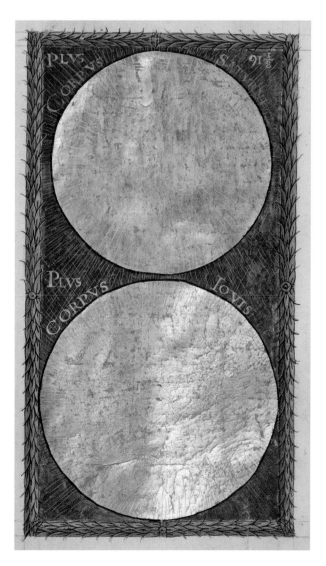

TYCHO BRAHE, COMET, 1577

Tycho Brahe's illustration of the comet of 1577 was first published in 1588 in his book *De Mundi Aetherei Recentioribus Phaenomenis Liber Secundus* (*Second Book About Recent Phenomena in the Celestial World*). In keeping with Tycho's cosmological model, Venus and Mercury orbit the Sun (C), which in turn orbits the Earth (A). He shows the new comet (X) in orbit around the Sun but outside the orbits of Mercury and Venus. When the comet is observed, it is closer to Earth than the planets or Sun, but further away than the Moon.

Finding by parallax that the comet lay far beyond the Moon, Tycho challenged the Aristotelian–Ptolemaic model of the universe. But by giving the comet a circular orbit around the Sun, Tycho at least preserved Aristotle's requirement for perfect circular movement beyond the sphere of the Moon.

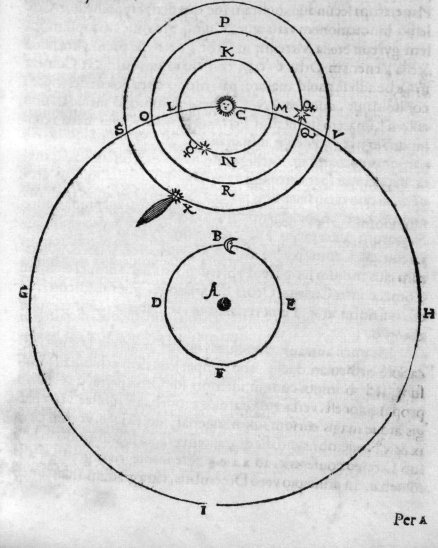

JOHANNES KEPLER, GEOMETRY OF THE SOLAR SYSTEM, 1596

Johannes Kepler published his first account of the solar system in *Mysterium Cosmographicum* (*The Cosmographic Mystery*) in 1596. It was the result of his work with distances and proportions in the Copernican model of the solar system. In it he presented a curious model of nested solids which he found mathematically defined the orbits of the planets. Kepler's was the first model to state the literal truth of Copernicus's heliocentric theory.

Kepler discovered that if he arranged the five Platonic solids in the right order, drawing spheres between them that exactly enclosed or were enclosed by the solids, the relative sizes of the resulting six spheres corresponded to the orbits of the six known planets. Moving out from the Sun, the solids appeared in the sequence: octahedron, icosahedron, dodecahedron, tetrahedron, cube. Because the model did not fit the observed data, Kepler's tutor Michael Mästlin wrote to Tycho Brahe hoping for better information. The result was that Kepler went to work with Brahe and later used his data to discover the elliptical orbits of the planets.

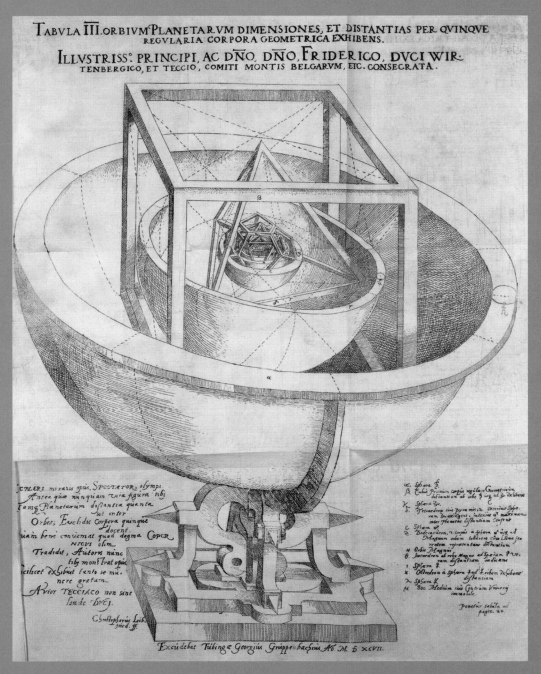

CHRISTOPH SCHEINER, SUNSPOTS, 1635

This colourized map was based on the work of the German Jesuit physicist Christoph Scheiner (1573–1650), who noticed sunspots in 1611 and entered into a dispute with Galileo about them. Scheiner supported the idea of the perfect heavens and tried to dismiss the spots as shadows cast on the Sun's surface by passing planets inside the orbit of Mercury. Eventually he was forced to change his view and accept the implied imperfection of the Sun. (Sunspots had already been noticed by ancient Chinese astronomers and, more recently, by Thomas Harriot and the father-and-son team David and Johannes Fabricius before either Scheiner or Galileo saw them.)

This map was included in *Mundus Subterraneus*, Athanasius Kircher's book on the geology of the Earth, published in 1664–5. As sunspots are transient, any attempt to map them is only a snapshot of the Sun's activity. Labels on the map indicate the solar axis, equator, north and south polar regions, the central equatorial region, sunspots (A), and solar prominences or flares (shown as puffs).

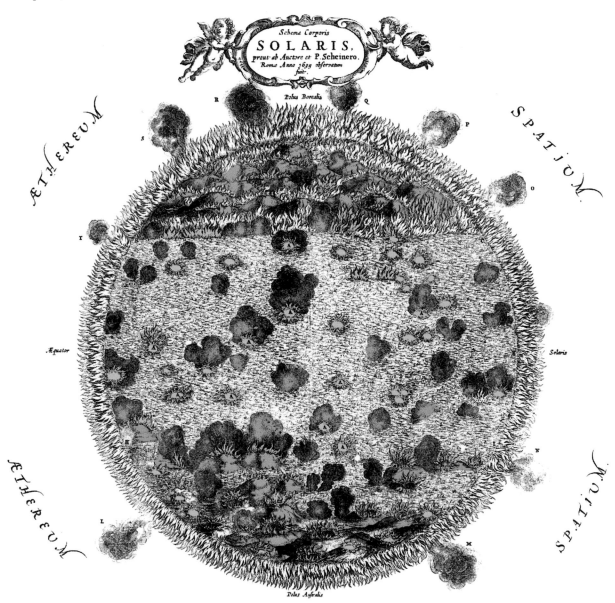

RENÉ DESCARTES, STELLAR VORTICES, 1644

The French philosopher René Descartes published his theory about the organization of the universe in *Principia philosophiae* (*The Principles of Philosophy*) in 1644. He believed that the universe is filled with matter – there is no void. According to Descartes, the matter whirls around in vortices, each centred on a star. The planets are caught in the whirling vortex so are in perpetual orbit around a star. Vortices are jammed up against one another. Our Sun is one among many stars, and the planets of our solar system are trapped within its vortex. All star–vortex compounds potentially have their own planetary systems in Descartes' model.

As is clear from the illustration, the vortices are differently oriented. Matter moves pole to pole in each vortex; in some this means matter is going into the plane of the page, while others are viewed face on, so we see the circle in its entirety.

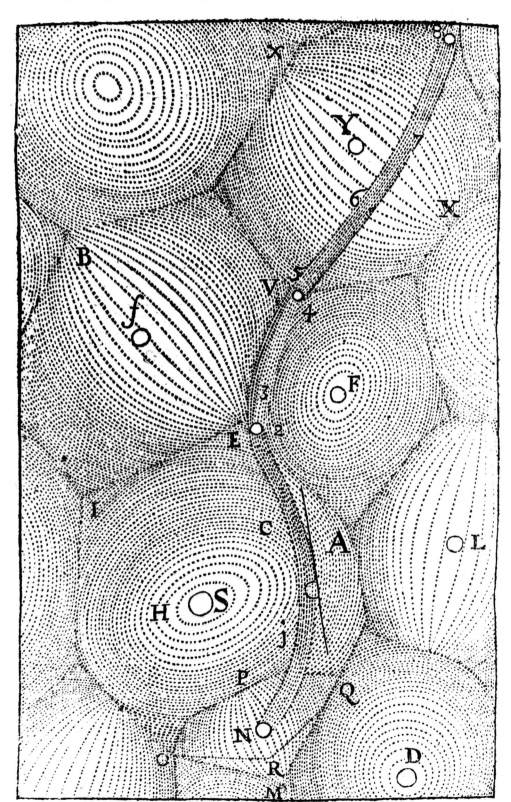

LEONHARD EULER, SOLAR SYSTEM AND COMETS, 1744

The German mathematician Leonhard Euler
untangled some of the mathematics of astronomy,
including accurately calculating the orbit of planets.
This diagram from *Theoria Motuum Planetarum et
Cometarum* (*The Theory of Motion of Planets and
Comets*) shows the solar system as one among many
in the galaxy. Our solar system shows moons orbiting
both Jupiter and Saturn, and a comet on a parabolic
path around the Sun.

CHARLES MESSIER, THE PATH OF A COMET, 1781

The French astronomer Charles Messier set out to plot the paths of comets
and to identify as many as he could. This chart shows the path taken by
comet Bode (C/1779 A1) that visited in 1779, shown against the background
sky. The comet charts (this is one of many) incidentally give an up-to-date
star chart.

Messier also made a catalogue of 'nebulous objects' (fuzzy, cloud-like
smears of light). His main purpose was to exclude them from consideration
as comets, which he could do if he knew where they were, as they were
fixed and comets are not. The area of Virgo (bottom right) shows as
nebulous objects some of the other galaxies in the Virgo super-cluster (of
which the Milky Way is a part). This chart records the position of asteroid
2 Pallas, undiscovered at this point; it is the earliest known record of an
asteroid observation.

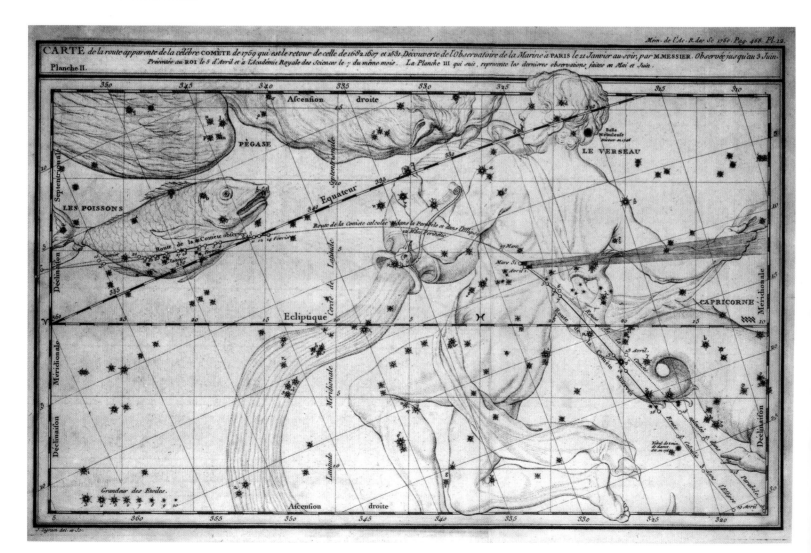

ÉTIENNE TROUVELOT, SOLAR FLARES, 1882

The artist Étienne Trouvelot, who produced beautiful drawings of the Moon (see page 64), also observed the Sun. His images of 'solar protuberances' capture transient but typical features, flares that leap from the surface of the Sun, emitting energy in virtually the entire electromagnetic spectrum. They were first seen in 1859 by an English amateur astronomer, Richard Carrington, who projected an image from an optical telescope through a broad-band filter. Solar flares can be seven times the size of the Earth.

Trouvelot also first observed and named veiled spots, grey areas which indicate either that a sunspot has been present but faded, or that a spot or group of spots is about to appear. They look like greyish patches and most often occur near the poles or the very centre of the disc of the Sun. Similar features, called 'wisps', are long streamers of grey haze.

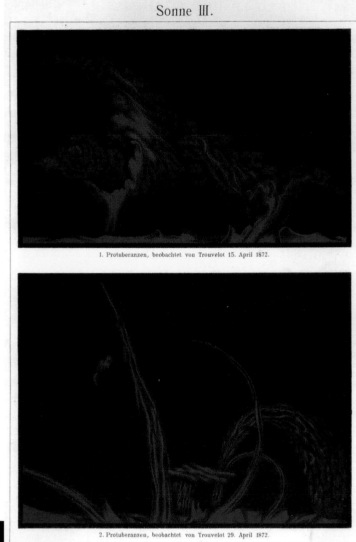

Sonne III.

1. Protuberanzen, beobachtet von Trouvelot 15. April 1872.

2. Protuberanzen, beobachtet von Trouvelot 29. April 1872.

Meyers Konv. - Lexikon, 6. Aufl.   Bibliograph. Institut, Leipzig.   *Zum Artikel „Sonne".*

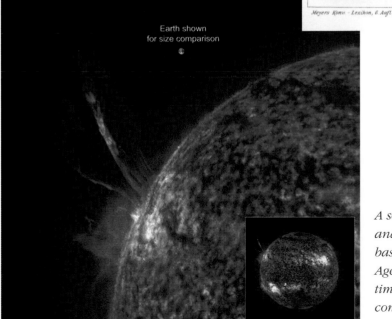

Earth shown for size comparison

A solar flare photographed in 1999 by the Solar and Heliospheric Observatory (SOHO), a space-based telescope operated by the European Space Agency and trained on the Sun. The flare is many times the size of the Earth (shown in white for comparison) and at 70,000 degrees Celsius is much hotter than the surface of the Sun.

SPECTRA OF THE SUN, 1895

The discovery that elements produce specific spectra by absorbing and reflecting different parts of the electromagnetic spectrum revolutionized investigation of the Sun and stars. This image shows the absorption and emission spectra of the Sun (top) and then of several elements, as determined by Robert Bunsen and Gustav Kirchhoff in 1859. Their discovery that spectra produced by the Sun match those of some known elements was the first evidence that the Sun and stars are made of the same chemical elements as the Earth – not some aether or other substance. The main constituents of the Sun are hydrogen and helium. Helium was first discovered in 1868, identified by its spectral signature in sunlight, and was only later found on Earth.

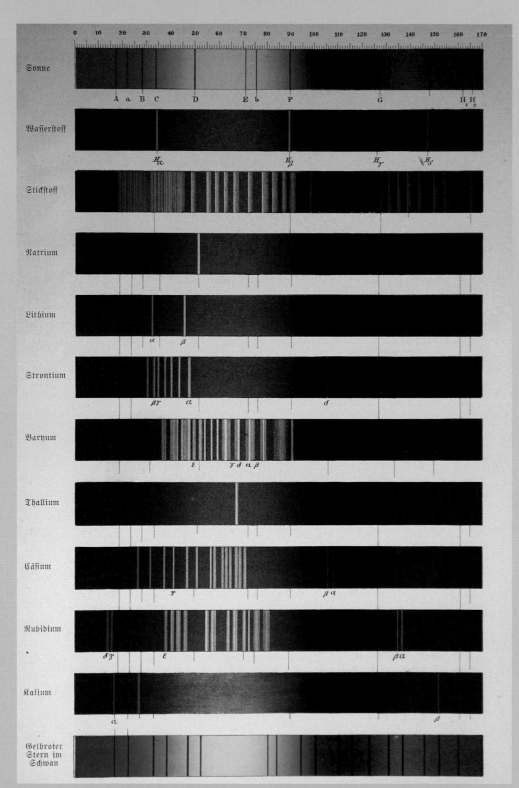

COMET CHURYUMOV-GERASIMENKO, ESA, 2015

This map of the comet 67P/Churyumov-Gerasimenko was produced from images and data collected by the European Space Agency's Rosetta spacecraft. Launched in 2004, Rosetta carried equipment and a lander, Philae, to map and study the surface and interior of the comet. Churyumov-Gerasimenko only measures 3.5 x 4km (2.2 x 2.5 miles) and consists of two lobes connected by a 'neck'. The areas of the comet have been named after Ancient Egyptian deities, such as Anubis, Seth, Atum, Hapi, Anuket, Babi, Ash, Ma'at, Serqet and Maftet. Unlike most mapping missions which are set up to examine a particular target, the Rosetta Mission was planned before a target comet was selected. Initial surveying and mapping of Churyumov-Gerasimenko had to be carried out very quickly, as the information was needed to select a landing site for Philae.

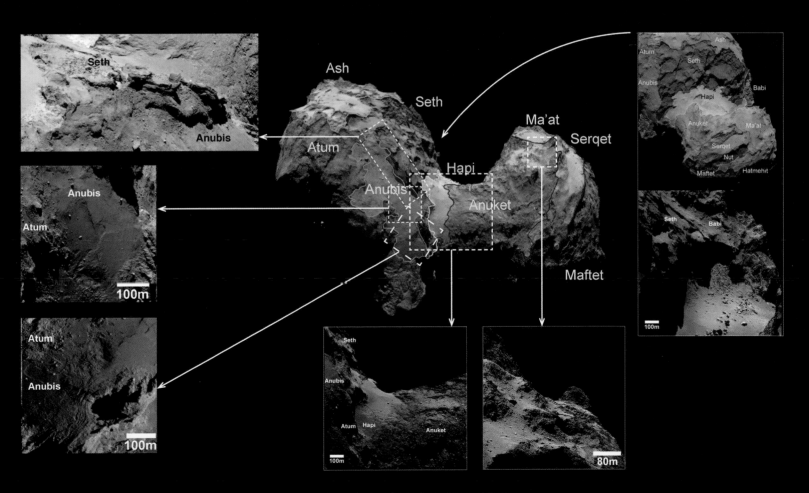

ESA/Rosetta/MPS for OSIRIS Team MPS/UPD/LAM/IAA/SSO/INTA/UPM/DASP/IDA

TWINKLE, TWINKLE

FROM TINY SPOTS TO DISTANT SUNS

IF YOU LOOK UP AT THE SKY, THE STARS ARE A bewildering array of randomly positioned spots of light, some brighter than others. It's easy to imagine they are dotted across the surface of a hemisphere which arches above us, and this is what they were first assumed to be. But that is far from the case. We now know that stars are scattered in three dimensions, some near, some unimaginably distant. As our telescopes have improved, we have found the stars receding ever further into the distance of possibly infinite space.

SEEING STARS

How do we map a collection of dots that have no logic or clear connection with one another? One way is to render them less random by making pictures from them, joining the dots. As the human brain is attuned to recognizing meaningful images and patterns, this makes them easier to visualize and remember. Another method is to use a coordinate system so that we can identify a star's position mathematically. But this approach is complicated by the fact that the stars seem to circle the celestial pole over the course of the night, so their position is time-dependent. Eventually, we ended up using both systems together.

Humans have been seeing pictures in the stars for millennia, though there are no surviving images of the earliest constellations described. The Ancient Greek writers Hesiod and Homer referred to patterns in the stars in the 8th century BC. The earliest known descriptions of star pictures were in the work of Eudoxus in the 4th century BC (now lost in its original form but preserved in a versified version) and *Phaenomena*, written around 275BC by Aratus (see page 24).

The dots to the right of the auroch's head in this cave painting at Lascaux, France, have been identified as the Pleiades star cluster within the Taurus constellation. The cave paintings at Lascaux date from 17,000BC.

It's likely that the Greek asterisms (the astronomical term for constellations) drew on the traditions of Egypt and Mesopotamia, probably developed around 1300–1100BC. Of the 48 Classical Greek constellations, 20 are shared with the Mesopotamian tradition, ten have the same groups of stars in different pictures and 18 are new, reflecting Greek interests and mythology. Sadly, no contemporary maps of the Greek and Mesopotamian constellations survive. Assyrian records from Mesopotamia are preserved on clay tablets, which include many astronomical texts but no pictures. As far as we know, the Greek-Egyptian astronomer Ptolemy did not draw his constellations. The earliest pictorial record of the Greek constellations is carved into the surface of the celestial globe carried by a marble statue of the Titan Atlas (see page 137).

Constellations provide one way of identifying and locating stars. It's easy to say 'the star in the middle of Orion's belt', to help someone to find it. But in his catalogue of 850 stars the Greek astronomer Hipparchus used a different method, a coordinate system based on celestial latitude and longitude centred on the ecliptic.

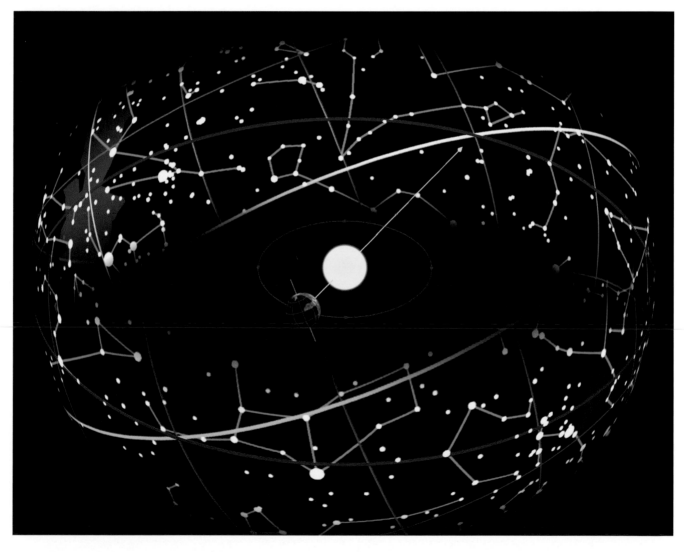

The ecliptic is the apparent path of the Sun against the background stars. The constellations of the zodiac are along the ecliptic.

The work of the Greek scholars passed into Islamic culture by way of Egypt under Greek and then Roman rule. After the Egyptian city of Alexandria was conquered by Muslim invaders in 641, Greek texts began to be translated into Arabic and the Greek constellations were integrated with the existing Arab constellations. Based in Bedouin tradition, the Arab method tended to name single stars or small groups rather than build pictures from many stars. Most stars were named after people or domestic or familiar animals, but a few small constellations were named after inanimate objects. Islamic astronomers re-surveyed the sky, making new maps of the stars and often changing the names Ptolemy had given them. Some Arab names are still used – for example, Aldebaran is a contraction of Al Dabaran, meaning 'the follower'. These star names and constellations were collected by the astronomer al-Sufi in the 10th century in his *Book of Fixed Stars* (see page 142).

These pages from a 12th-century manuscript of al-Sufi's Book of Fixed Stars *describe the stars of the Corona Borealis (Northern Crown) on the left and give tabulated information about the stars of Boötes (The Herdsman) on the right.*

GOING SOUTH

The stars seen by Mesopotamian, Egyptian, Greek and Arab astronomers were those of the northern hemisphere. A whole host of stars greeted the first European explorers to venture into the southern hemisphere. The earliest star maps of the south, starting in the 16th century, show large tracts of sky with no constellations where the stars had not been mapped. Astronomers rushed to fill them with constellations of their own devising. There was some fluidity in the constellations of both northern and southern hemispheres as astronomers created new constellations that were sometimes recognized by their colleagues and successors, but sometimes not. Those existing briefly included the reindeer, the slug and the 'electric machine'.

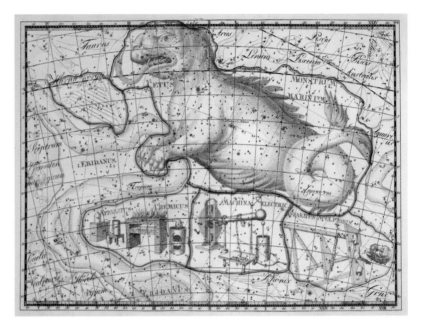

Machina electrica in Bode's Uranographia, *1801.*

As the telescope brought an increasing number of stars into view, it was not practical to try to fit these into more and more named asterisms – a new rigorous, extendable and rational method was needed. The coordinate system, the method used in terrestrial mapping for specifying locations, came into favour. But it did not entirely replace asterisms. The distinction between 'asterism' and 'constellation' has become important, as 'constellation' is now the official name for regions. The

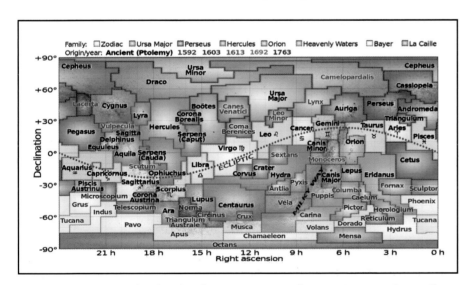

Modern astronomy divides the sky into 88 constellations, regions that still largely correspond with the Ancient Greek asterisms.

borders of the 88 constellations are laid down by the International Astronomical Union (IAU), still centred on constellations named by our star-gazing ancestors. The legacy of the Egyptians, Greeks and Arabs is present every day in the work of NASA and the great observatories of the world.

The north and south celestial poles (points directly above the North and South Poles) are important in locating stars, but these move over the course of centuries. The Earth's axis is tilted in relation to the plane of its orbit around the Sun. The axis itself is not fixed but traces out a circle over a period of 26,000 years, leading to a phenomenon known as precession. Consequently, the celestial poles move, 'pointing at' slightly different areas of the sky as time passes. There is a star above the North Pole at the moment, but not above the South Pole. Over 26,000 years, different stars take their turn as pole star (and sometimes a region of empty space has a turn). Although precession is on a very long cycle, enough time has passed since the earliest astronomical records were made for it to have had an effect on the way in which the night sky is depicted, so early star atlases no longer exactly match the stars we see.

ORION, GEISSENKLÖSTERLE IVORY PLATE, 33,000–30,000BC

This carved piece of mammoth ivory was discovered in a collapsed cave complex in Geissenklösterle, Germany. One side (left) shows a human or partly human figure, taken to represent Orion. This would make it the earliest known depiction of an asterism. The proportions correspond to the positions of the stars that make up Orion as they were 32,000 years ago. The other side of the piece holds a series of pits and notches which might have been used as some form of calendar.

   We can't know if or how this object fitted into a Paleolithic cosmology, but its very existence, if it has been correctly interpreted, shows that our distant ancestors were already seeing figures in the patterns of the stars and perhaps making up stories to go with them.

NEBRA SKY DISC, *c.*1600BC

A Bronze Age disc found by treasure looters in Germany in 1999 shows the circle of the Sun or full moon, a crescent moon four or five days old, and a group of dots that matches the Pleiades star cluster as it appeared 3,600 years ago. The disc was seized from black-market dealers by the German police in 2002. Its use remained a puzzle until 2006, when German researchers found that it corresponds to instructions in a Babylonian tablet text known as MUL.APIN. These explain how to calculate when to add an extra (intercalary) month to the calendar to realign the lunar cycle and the annual solar sequence.

The disc is made of bronze, the green colouring achieved by adding a rotten-egg mixture to the metal. The astronomical features attached to the surface are in gold leaf.

SARCOPHAGUS HALL, TOMB OF SETI I, 1305–1290BC

The 'astronomical ceiling' in the empty sarcophagus hall of the tomb of Seti I of Ancient Egypt features the oldest known example of this type of Egyptian astronomical diagram. This image, part of the northern half, shows deities and their associated constellations, and a list of the decanal stars (36 stars that rose above the horizon in sequence over the course of a year). The constellations shown include Meskhetyu (the Plough/Big Dipper) in the fourth column from the left.

FARNESE ATLAS, 2ND CENTURY

The Farnese Atlas is a Roman statue made in the 2nd century AD; it's a copy of an earlier Greek work. The Titan Atlas supports a celestial globe on his shoulders, depicting 41 constellations. Atlas was condemned to stand at the western edge of the world (Gaia), holding up the sky for all eternity. This harsh sentence was punishment for siding with the Titans in their war against the Olympians.

The celestial globe is quite accurate, and historians of astronomy have suggested the positions of the constellations indicate that the original might have been based on the star catalogue of Hipparchus, compiled 129BC. The Farnese Atlas is the only pictorial representation of the Greek constellations to have survived; they were next depicted in al-Sufi's *Book of Fixed Stars* (see page 142).

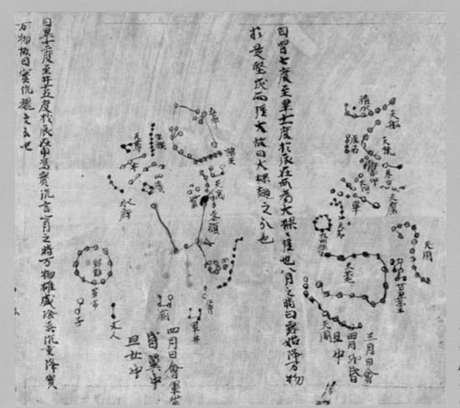

The image on the left shows the Orion constellation. On the page opposite, the northern polar region can be seen, with the Big Dipper in the lower half of the map.

THE DUNHUANG STAR ATLAS, AD705–10

The world's oldest star atlas is painted on a scroll, created during the Tang Dynasty (618–907) in China. It depicts and names 1,339 stars in 257 asterisms covering all the northern hemisphere visible from China. The constellations were derived from star catalogues compiled by previous astronomers, and the stars are colour-coded to show their provenance. Stars associated with Wu Xian are shown in white and/or yellow; those associated with Gan De are in black; those of Shi Shen are shown in red. Gan De and Shi Shen were contemporaries in the 4th century BC, but the stars assigned to Shi Shen match the sky around 100BC. Wu Xian lived during the Shang Dynasty, *c.*1600–1046BC, and was a shaman. His name is associated with the catalogue, but there is no other record of astronomical work by him.

The scroll containing the star charts was discovered in the Mogao Caves near Dunhuang in 1907. The cave had been walled up and hidden for 1,000 years; it yielded more than 40,000 manuscripts, paintings and printed documents on various subjects.

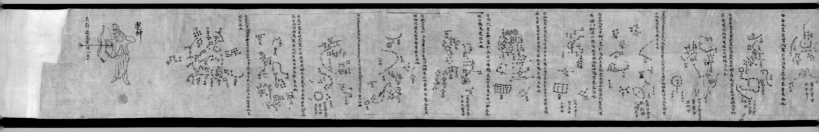

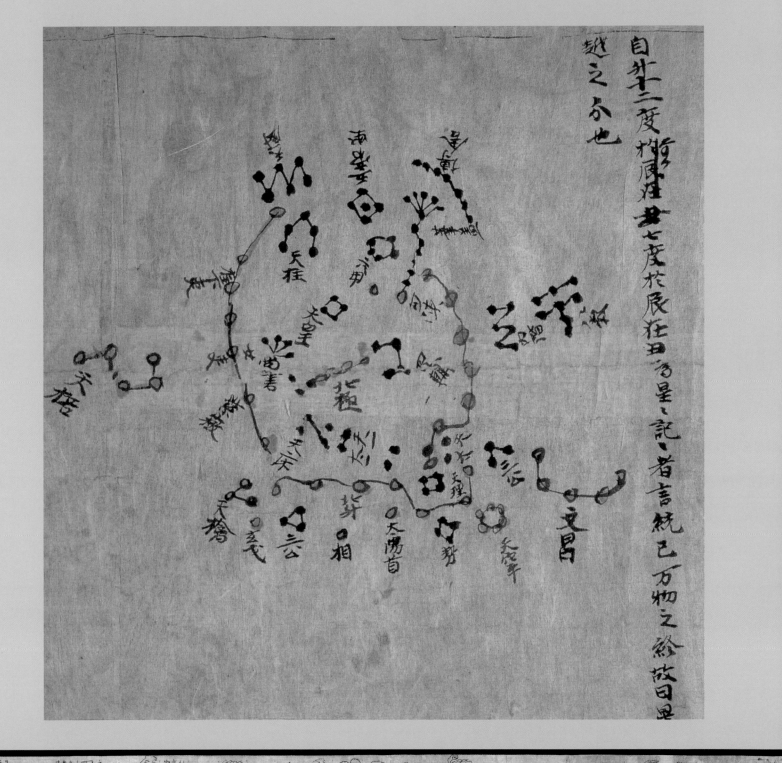

LEIDEN *ARATEA*, *c.*816

The Leiden *Aratea* is a copy of the Latin translation of the *Phaenomena* of Aratus (see page 24). It is a poem about the stars, illustrated with beautiful images of the constellations. The positions of the stars are not accurate, the artist being more interested in the mythological figures than the asterisms to which they correspond. Strictly speaking this is not a star map as the positions are not given with sufficient rigour for anyone to locate the stars accurately. However, it is as close as 9th-century Europe came to star mapping. The artist presents 43 constellations, some seen as they are when we look up at the sky and some viewed from behind, as they would appear on a celestial globe (known as an exterior view).

The image on the left shows the constellation Draco accompanied by Ursa Major and Ursa Minor; the one at the top shows Delphinus.

CICERO, TRANSLATION OF ARATUS' *PHAENOMENA*, 9TH–11TH CENTURY

Another version of *Phaenomena*, this time translated by Cicero, is preserved in a manuscript collection of astronomical texts. The constellations are represented by their figures, which are filled with text describing their mythological significance. This image shows Pisces, the fish.

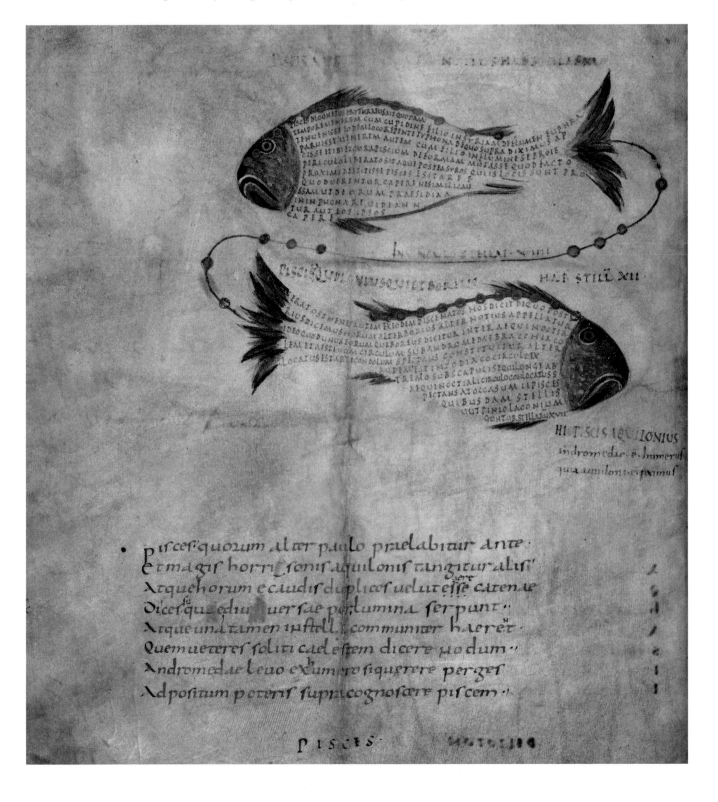

AL-SUFI, *THE BOOK OF FIXED STARS*, 964 (1009 COPY)

When the Persian astronomer Abd al-Rahman al-Sufi wrote *The Book of Fixed Stars* in 964, his aim was to combine the star catalogue in Ptolemy's *Almagest* with the local Arab (Berber) astronomical tradition. The book lists 1,018 stars, giving their approximate positions, magnitudes and colours. It contains the earliest account of the Andromeda Galaxy, which al-Sufi called a 'little cloud', and represents the first description of another galaxy.

The work illustrates each of the constellations separately and shows them in two views – as they appear when we look up, and an exterior view. The original book has been lost. The earliest surviving copy, from 1009, was compiled by al-Sufi's son.

The stars marked in red are those included in the constellation, and other stars are given for context. When the Arabic version of Ptolemy's work was translated in Spain around 1250, al-Sufi's illustrated maps were included with it. His drawings became templates for the outlines of the constellations until the Renaissance. This image shows the constellation of Gemini, the twins.

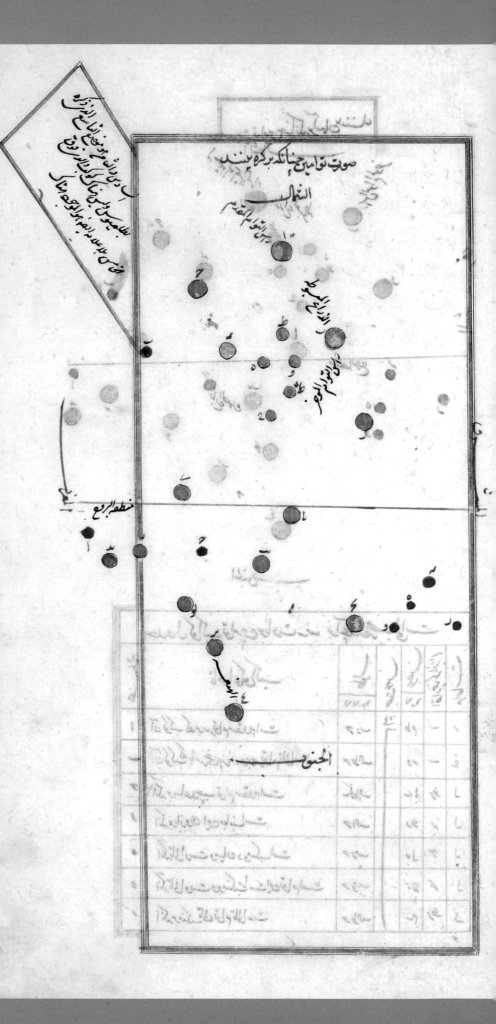

HUANG SHANG, SUZHOU PLANISPHERE, 1193

The astronomer Huang Shang created a star chart in 1193 which was carved in stone in 1247 by Wang Zhiyuan. This print was taken from the stone in 1826. It is a planispheric depiction of the stars of the northern hemisphere, centred on the north celestial pole, though at the time the map was made there was no star in the polar position (see page 133), and the current Pole Star is five degrees from the celestial pole.

The lines radiating from the inner circle divide the sky into the 28 lunar mansions. The start of each lunar mansion is marked by a star on its boundary with the last. The position of any star in the sky is specified by giving the distance from the Pole Star and from the western starting point of the mansion in which it is located.

The inscription says there are 283 asterisms containing a total of 1,563 stars, but there appear to be only 1,436 stars. The Milky Way, shown in outline, is called the 'River of Heaven' in Chinese astronomy. The planisphere shows virtually all the stars visible to the naked eye from China.

IMAD AL-DIN MAHMUD AL-KASHI, HOROSCOPE OF PRINCE ISKANDAR, 1411

This horoscope shows the state of the heavens on 25 April 1384, the birth date of the Timurid prince Iskandar, grandson of Emperor Tamerlane the Great. It was created in 1411, the second year of Iskandar's rule and four years before his early death. Around the central zodiac, four angels carry golden gifts for the young prince. In the central circle, Mars (in the eleventh house) is shown as a warrior carrying a sword in one hand and a severed head in the other. The book was produced by the royal *kitabkhana*, or publishing house, bringing together the skills of astronomers, illuminators, gilders, calligraphers and expert paper- and book-makers.

HYGINUS' *POETICON ASTRONOMICON*, 1482

De astronomica, or *Poeticon astronomicon*, was probably written in the 2nd century AD by a Roman writer called Hyginus. It retells the myths that relate to 47 of the 48 constellations recognized by Ptolemy. The first published edition, from which these illustrations are taken, was produced in Venice in 1482 and contains some of the earliest printed depictions of constellations. It uses legend to account for the patterns of the stars and shows how mythical history is enacted in the juxtapositions of some of the constellations.

These pages show the constellations Cassiopeia (left) and Andromeda (right). Hyginus writes of Andromeda: 'They say she was put among the constellations by the favour of Minerva, on account of the valour of Perseus, who freed her from danger when exposed to the sea-monster. Nor did he receive less kindness from her in return for his good deed. For neither her father Cepheus nor her mother Cassiopeia could dissuade her from following Perseus, leaving parents and country. About her Euripides has written a most excellent play with her name as title.'

Andromeda is, strangely, depicted as a hermaphrodite. This might result from confusion on the part of the illustrator as Perseus, who saved her, was sometimes considered a hermaphrodite. In his poem 'Andromeda Liberata' George Chapman (1614) describes her: 'Amongst the fairest women you could finde/Then Perseus, none more faire; mongst worthiest men,/No one more manly: . . . Such was the halfe-divine-borne Trojan Terror/Where both Sex graces met as in their Mirror.'

In the illustration at the bottom of the page, Hydra, the water snake, is shown with two other constellations – Corvus (the crow), which sits on Hydra's back, and Crater (the cup or bowl). The reason Hyginus gives for this arrangement of constellations is as follows: the god Apollo sent the crow to fetch some pure water from a spring, but on its way the bird spotted a fig tree and perched in the branches to wait for the fruit to ripen. After several days, when the figs had ripened and the crow had eaten them, it returned with a bowl of water. Apollo, angry that he had been forced to use other water while the crow delayed, inflicted a punishment upon it. From then on, throughout the period while the figs were ripening, the crow was unable to drink. Apollo set the water snake in the heavens to guard the bowl from the thirsty crow. The crow pecks at the snake's tail to try to reach the water, but to no avail.

Ndromeda ppe caſſiopēiā ſupꝛa caput perſei bꝛcui
iteruallo oiſſidēte pſpicif collocata:manib⁹ oſuerſis
vincta vt antiquis biſtoꝛiis ē traditū: cui⁹ caput eq̄
pegaſi vētri coniungif.Eadē eni itella vt vmbilicus
pegaſi ꝛ andromedę caput appellaf. bui⁹ medium
pect⁹ ꝛ manū ſiniſtrā circul⁹ eſtiuus oiuidit. Occidit autē cū piſce
oe ouobus ſecūdo:quē andromedę ſubiectū bꝛachio ſupꝛa oiꝛi/
mus. Exoꝛiēte libꝛa ꝛ ſcoꝛpione capite pꝛiuſq̄ reliquo coꝛpe pue/
nit ad terrā. Exoꝛif autē cū piſcib⁹ ꝛ ariete . bęc vt ſupꝛa oiximus
babet i capite ſtellā clare lucentē vnā. In vtroqꝛ bumero vnā. In
cubito oextro vnā. In ipſa manu vnam . In ſiniſtro cubito vel in

Andromeda

Idra trium ſignoꝛum longitudinē occupans cancri
leonis ꝛ virginis:inter equinoctialē circulum ꝛ bye
malem collocatur: Ita tamen vt caput eius con/
tendens ad ſignū id quod pꝛocyon vocaf:ꝛ totius
bydrę pꝛoꝑie quarta pars inter eſtiuū ꝛ equinoctia/
lē circulū videaf. Lauda aūt extrema pene cētauri caput tegēt: ſu/
ſtinet in oorſo coꝛui:roſtro corpus eius tangētē ꝛ toto coꝛpoꝛe
ad craterem tendentē:qui ſatis longo oiſcidente interuallo pꝛope
nter leonem ꝛ virginem conſtitutus videtur inclinatior ad caput

hydra

f 4

ALBRECHT DÜRER, *IMAGINES COELI*, 1515

The great painter and printer Albrecht Dürer produced the first printed
star chart in Europe, published in 1515. The constellations of the zodiac
are reversed and progress counterclockwise, as on a celestial globe (so
presenting an exterior, God's-eye view of the sky). This was the first celestial
atlas in the style that would become typical of the Renaissance. Dürer
replaced the al-Sufi styled figures with ones based in Classical tradition, with
nudity and togas replacing Arab dress and turbans. It was a style that would
endure for 200 years.

The positions of the stars are remarkably accurate. Dürer worked with talented collaborators. Johannes Stabius, imperial astronomer at the court of Maximilian I in Vienna, designed the projection and provided the coordinate system. The astronomer and mathematician Konrad Heinfogel indicated the positions of the stars, updated from the star catalogue in Ptolemy's *Almagest*.

The lines drawn at 30 degrees radiating from the celestial pole and the figures around the rim allow the positions of the stars to be located easily, and represent the beginnings of a coordinate system. Unfortunately, as the constellations present a mirror image of what is seen looking at the sky and there is no indication of a star's magnitude, they were difficult to use as star maps. The large blank areas of the southern hemisphere don't signify an absence of stars there; they were left like this because Europeans knew of no constellations made up from the stars in this region.

PETER APIAN AND MICHAEL OSTENDORFER, *ASTRONOMICUM CAESAREUM*, 1540

The *Astronomicum Caesareum*, published in 1540 by Peter Apian, is an early pop-up book composed of paper engineering elements which demonstrate the ingenuity of the astrolabe, an instrument used for finding the positions of heavenly bodies. It was compiled by Michael Ostendorfer, official astronomer to Holy Roman Emperor Charles V. Peter Apian pioneered producing books with moving parts, called 'volvelles'. Of the 55 leaves, 21 have moving parts. The index strings were originally adorned with seed pearls.

Actual astrolabes were made of metal, like this Indo-Persian brass example made around 1601. It consists of a back plate marked around the edge with degrees, overlaid with a plate engraved with circles of celestial latitude and altitude and then a filigree-like fretwork (called the rete) indicating the positions of bright stars. The user needs to know the altitude of a reference star, then turns the rete until that star is lined up at the correct altitude on the plate. The positions of other stars can then be read off.

ALESSANDRO PICCOLOMINI, *DE LE STELLE FISSE*, 1540

Alessandro Piccolomini wrote the first printed star atlas. His book, *De le Stelle Fisse* (*Of the Fixed Stars*) presented clear pictures of the stars without drawing the associated figures of the constellations, although it included their mythological descriptions. Piccolomini introduced a system using Roman letters to show the magnitude of the stars, with 'a' the brightest, 'b' the second brightest, and so on. The size of the star also related to its brightness; a scale at the foot of the page helped to indicate the size of the constellation. The text described approximately where to look in relation to the celestial pole – so

'*parte verso il polo*' tells the reader to look to the left of the celestial pole. This page shows the constellation Lepus (the Hare).

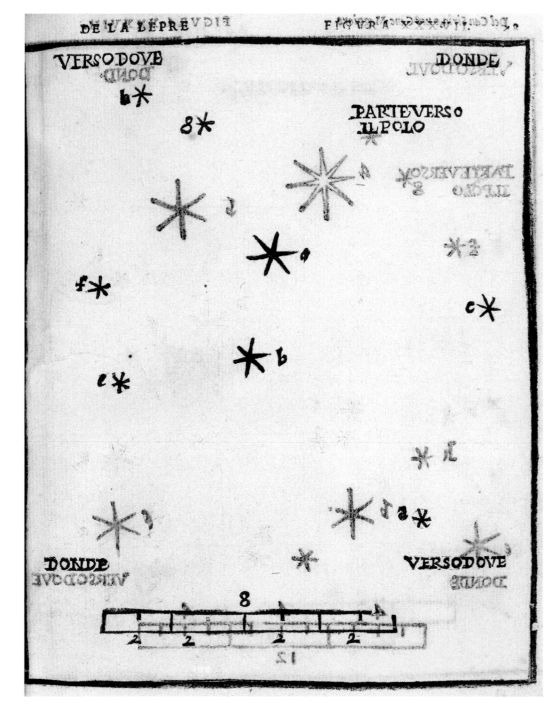

JOHANN BAYER, *URANOMETRIA*, 1624

Bayer's *Uranometria* was one of the most important star atlases ever published – and the first major star atlas printed in Europe. Produced in Augsburg, Germany, in 1603, it went through eight editions between 1624 and 1689. Although all printing was in black and white at the time, the plates in this and many other early books were often hand-coloured after printing.

Uranometria contained plates for each of the 48 Ptolemaic constellations and in later editions included the twelve new constellations of the southern sky (image below). These were devised by Petrus Plancius from the stars reported following the first Dutch trading expedition to the East Indies. Plancius styled most of his constellations after the natural world, but made exceptions for the hydra, the phoenix and the Triangulum Australe.

Bayer took 1,005 star positions from Tycho Brahe's tables and augmented them with 1,000 of his own observations. The result was an atlas which contained more stars than any previously. The band of the Milky Way is visible across both northern and southern celestial hemispheres.

Each plate has a grid and the margins are calibrated in degrees, allowing very accurate coordinate positions to be read. Although the star positions are shown as they are seen from Earth, the figures of the constellations are shown in exterior view, so are mirror images of the star patterns. This means the positions of the stars don't match their usual locations in the constellations – for example, the star that would be in Orion's left foot is in his right. This page shows the constellation Hydra.

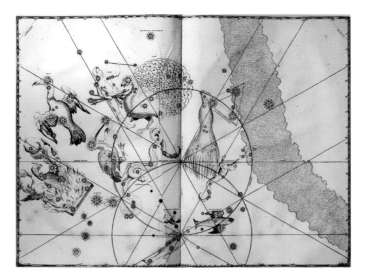

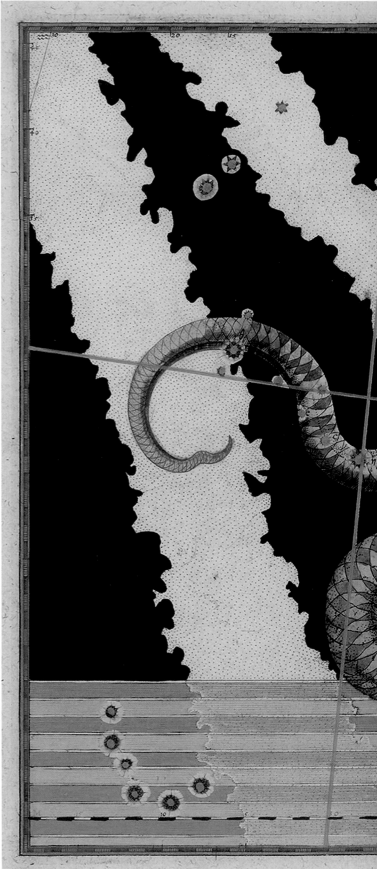

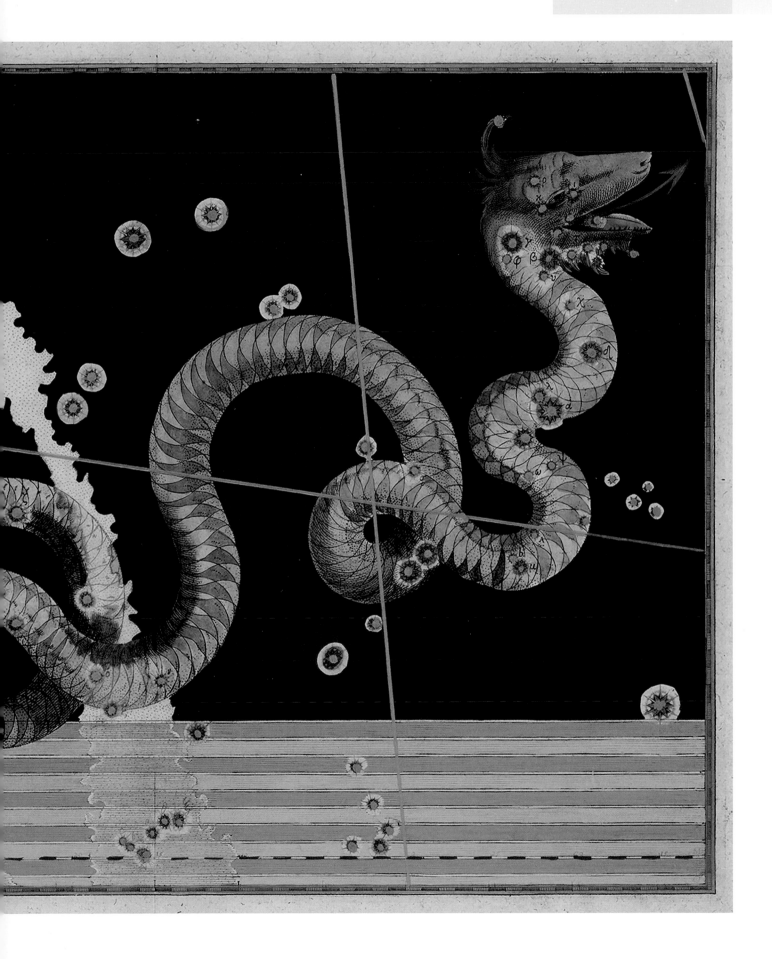

ANDREAS CELLARIUS, CLASSICAL CONSTELLATIONS OF THE NORTHERN HEMISPHERE, 1660

Gerard Mercator's *Chronologica* (see page 37) was an ambitious attempt to cover all the known cosmos and the complete history of the Earth. He died before completing it, and it took 100 years for the last volumes to appear, produced by others (including Cellarius). The final volume, *Harmonia Macrocosmica*, depicts the three theoretical arrangements of the cosmos of the time: the Ptolemaic, the Copernican and Tycho Brahe's in-between version (see pages 40–41). Similarly, it depicts both the pagan and a Christianized version of the constellations (see page 156). The one shown here is the traditional representation of the sky of the northern hemisphere. The *Harmonia* goes on to discuss general issues such as the nature of the Sun and Moon and the magnitude of the stars.

ANDREAS CELLARIUS, CHRISTIANIZED CONSTELLATIONS OF THE NORTHERN HEMISPHERE, 1660

Here, Cellarius presents the Christianized version of the constellations. The figures in the asterisms are drawn from biblical narratives or are early Christian figures and saints. The Christian constellations were first featured in Julius Schiller's *Coelum Stellatum Christianum*, published in 1627. Schiller replaced the constellations of the northern hemisphere with figures from New Testament narratives, those of the southern hemisphere with figures from Old Testament narratives, and the zodiacal constellations with the twelve apostles. Cellarius also linked the planets, Moon and Sun with biblical figures rather than classical deities.

STELLATI
ANI HÆ
RIUM PRIUS.

FREDERIK DE WIT, *CELESTIAL MAP, 1670*

Frederik de Wit was a Dutch cartographer, internationally renowned. He produced atlases, town plans and nautical charts as well as this stunning celestial map. It presents the cosmological models of Ptolemy, Copernicus and Brahe without stating a preference, but the depiction of the movement and illumination of the Earth (bottom right) uses the Copernican model with an orbital shape that suggests the influence of Kepler (though not accurately). The tilt of the Earth's axis is clearly shown in this diagram.

The main part of the chart shows the constellations of the northern and southern skies, with the figures and important stars named.

VINCENZO CORONELLI, GLOBES OF THE SUN KING, 1681–3

The two globes of the Sun King, one celestial and the other terrestrial, were made by Italian cartographer Vincenzo Coronelli between 1681 and 1683. They are each 4m (13ft) across. The celestial globe shows 72 constellations: the 48 identified by Ptolemy and additional constellations described more recently, including those of the southern hemisphere. The constellations are represented by their corresponding allegorical figures, each labelled in French, Latin, Greek and Arabic. The Sun slides along a metal bar which represents the ecliptic; 1,880 stars are marked by metal studs, their size relative to their brightness. Comets are shown with the date of their discovery.

A close-up of Monoceros (the Unicorn), a constellation at the celestial equator identified by Petrus Plancius in the 17th century.

JOHANNES HEVELIUS, *FIRMAMENTUM SOBIESCIANUM*, 1690

Polish astronomer Johannes Hevelius was somewhat old-fashioned, and insisted on carrying out all his observations with the naked eye despite the telescope having been in existence for more than half a century. His *Firmamentum Sobiescianum* was an atlas comprising two hemispheres and plates showing 73 constellations, some of which were new ones that he had invented himself. Most of the positions of the northern stars were based on his own observations, but he used Halley's data for 341 southern stars observed in 1676. Hevelius presented the constellations with external orientation, another old-fashioned twist, and he didn't label the stars in the maps but located them by describing their place in a constellation.

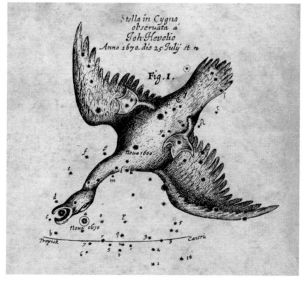

In 1670, a new star appeared, causing interest and consternation in astronomical circles. Johannes Hevelius showed its position in relation to the constellation Cygnus, the swan, calling it 'nova sub capite Cygni' ('new star below the head of the Swan'). The 'star', known as Nova Vulpeculae 1670, is now thought to have been a collision between two stars.

ERHARD WEIGEL, CELESTIAL GLOBE, 1699

Erhard Weigel was professor of mathematics at the University of Jena. His celestial globe aimed to replace the 'heathen' names of Greek, Islamic and Babylonian constellations with Christian, aristocratic, European ones. The globe is a curious and confusing mish-mash: the familiar constellations are painted on the surface, with the new constellations in relief on top of them. Each star is marked by a tiny hole. To make the stars 'shine', a light was placed inside the globe.

Weigel was responsible for another innovation in celestial globes, this time rather more successful. At the time, most globes presented an external view of the stars; while on Earth, of course, we see the stars on the inside of a hemisphere. In some of his celestial globes, Weigel cut one or more slightly larger holes so that the viewer could peer inside and see the constellations the right way round, as they appear from Earth.

PAWNEE SKY MAP, *c.*1700 OR EARLIER

This star chart on tanned deer skin was created by the Skiri Pawnee Native Americans, possibly 300 years ago. It was found in Pawnee, Oklahoma, in 1906. The chart is 38 x 55cm (15 x 21½in). Stars are shown as four-pointed crosses in five different sizes, corresponding to magnitude. The band of very small (lowest magnitude stars) across the middle represents the Milky Way, called the Spirit Path by the Pawnee. Just below the band, a circle of stars represents the Corona Borealis (Northern Crown); Polaris, the Pole Star, is just to the left of it.

The top of the chart shows stars best seen in winter and the bottom of the chart shows constellations seen in the summer. The stars were very important to the Pawnee, and the Pole Star and the Pleiades were particularly prominent in their mythology. The Pleiades are the closely packed group of six stars just above the Milky Way and below the largest stars at the top of the chart. The thick, bounding line around the chart represents the horizon.

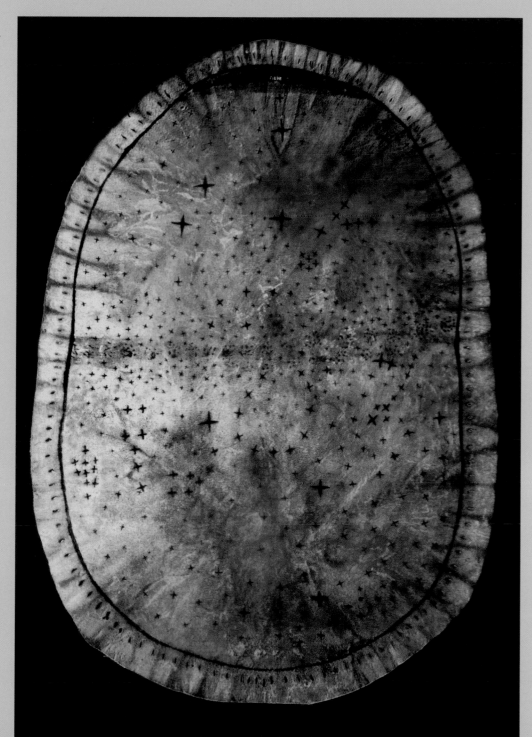

JOHN FLAMSTEED, *ATLAS COELESTIS*, 1729

John Flamsteed was an English astronomer and the first Astronomer Royal.
He was probably the first person to record the planet Uranus, though he didn't
recognize it as such and mistook it for a star. In 1729, ten years after Flamsteed's
death, his widow published a star atlas based on his observations. The atlas
was corrected in the 1770s to account for the slight movement of some of the
stars, and updated again in 1795. Nebulae not known in Flamsteed's time were
revealed by improved telescopes and included in later editions. Uranus was
identified as a planet in 1783.

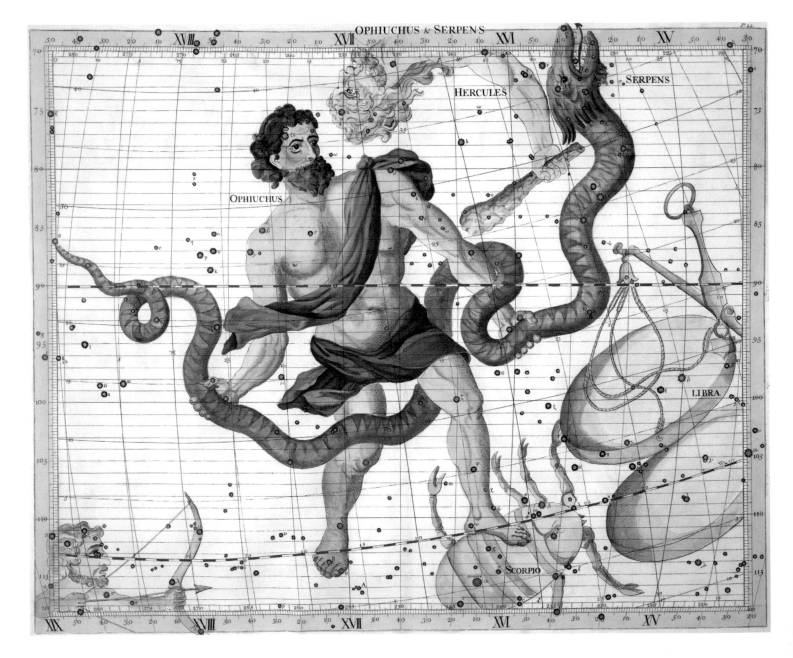

Flamsteed's atlas was based on his own observations and accurate measurements of the positions of the stars. In addition to the traditional grid based on the ecliptic, he used a new equatorial grid system, which was a projection of Earth's equator onto the sky. In its time, Flamsteed's atlas was the largest ever published and contained more stars than the atlases of Hevelius and Bayer.

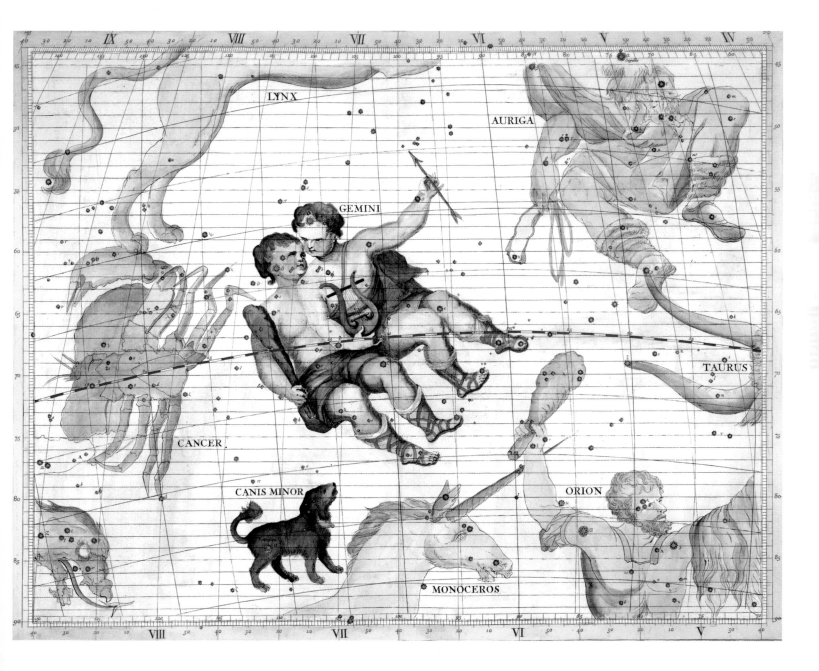

NICOLAS LOUIS DE LACAILLE, *COELUM AUSTRALE STELLIFERUM*, 1763

In 1750, Nicolas de Lacaille set sail from France for Cape Town, South Africa, and over the course of 1751–2 observed and mapped 9,800 stars of the southern hemisphere. He created 17 new constellations, 14 based on his observations in Cape Town and three created by breaking up the existing large constellation Argo Navis (the ship Argo). Using this method he filled the gaps left in the southern sky. Instead of naming the constellations after mythological figures, Lacaille used technological instruments and tools as his inspiration; his new names included the furnace (Fornax), the microscope (Microscopium), the compass (Pyxis) and the telescope (Telescopium). His constellations are still recognized today.

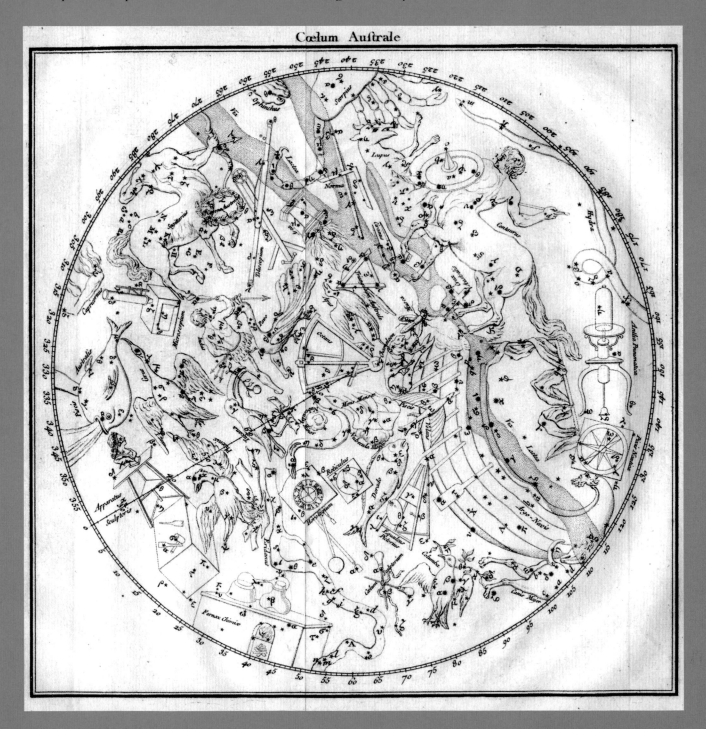

JOHANN SCHAUBACH, SOUTHERN STARS, *CATASTERISMI*, 1795

This map of the southern constellations was produced in Germany in 1795 to illustrate an edition of *Catasterismi*, written in the 1st century AD possibly by Eratosthenes of Cyrene. Catasterismi means 'placings among the stars', and the text gives the mythology behind the figures of the constellations. The illustration depicts the southern constellations known to the Ancient Greeks. There is a blank area around the South Pole as the ancients had never seen this part of the sky so had no constellations for it.

The map is centred on the geographic South Pole, with the ecliptic shown arching through the upper half of the map. The relative brightness of the stars is shown, with a scale at the bottom.

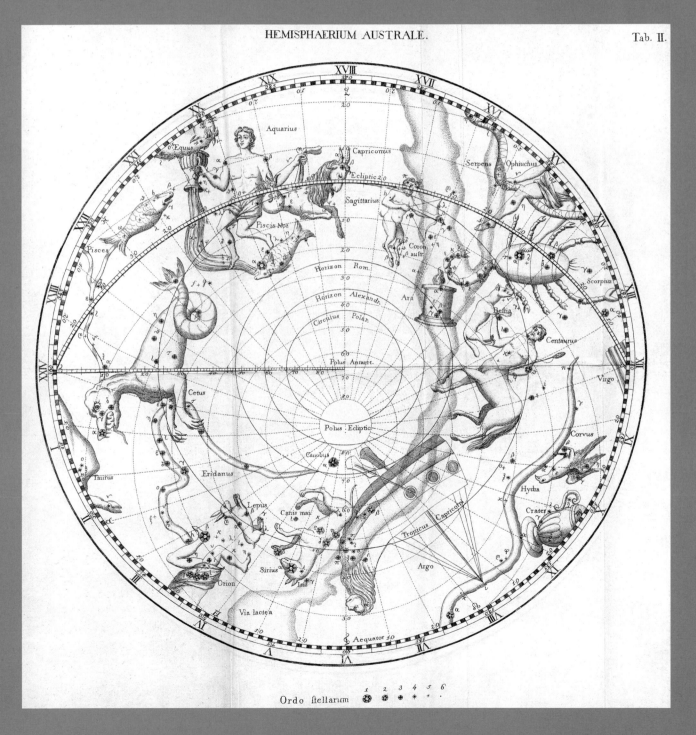

CHRISTOPH GOLDBACH AND FRANZ VON ZACH, GEMINI, 1799

The band of the Milky Way gives context to the constellation of Gemini or the Twins (*Zwillinge*), here picked out with star shapes. This map is from *Neuester Himmels-Atlas* by the German astronomers Christoph Friedrich Goldbach and Franz Xaver von Zach. It was based on a French abridged edition of Flamsteed's atlas published in 1795. The introduction specifies that it was intended to be especially useful to amateur and novice astronomers. The stars are shown in white against a black background to make it easier to compare the ones on the page with those in the sky.

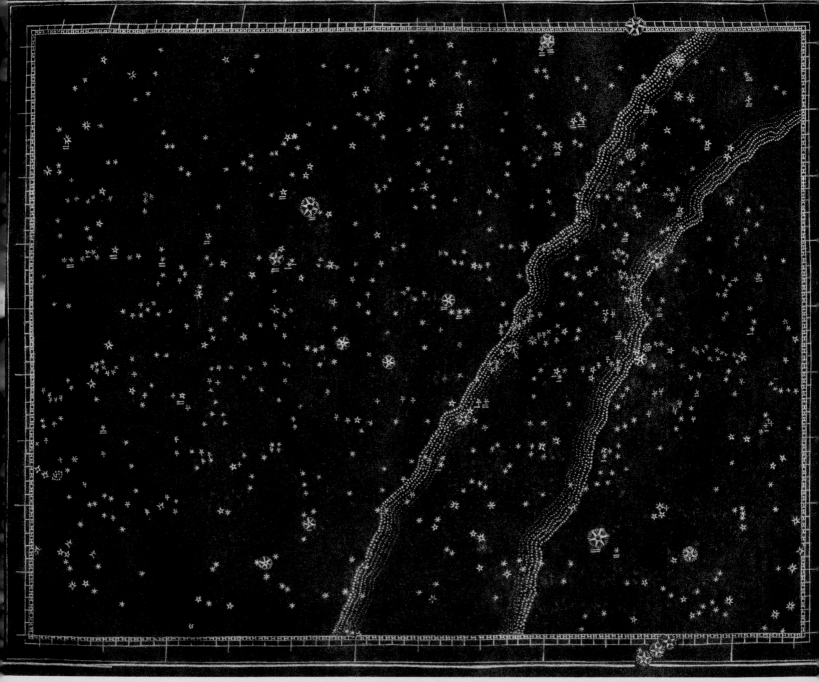

JOHANN BODE, *URANOGRAPHIA*, 1801

Johann Bode produced several important astronomy texts and established
a law that seemed to describe the space between planetary orbits, the
Titius–Bode law. His *Uranographia*, published in 1801, was the largest
and most comprehensive star atlas ever published, listing 17,240 stars and
2,500 nebulae – far more than any previous publication. It was the last great
pictorial star atlas.

WILLIAM CROSSWELL, MERCATOR STAR MAP, 1810

This map of the constellations was produced by the American cartographer William Crosswell and published in Boston in 1810. Two new constellations are included alongside the usual set, *Sciurus volans* ('flying squirrel', upper left) and *Marmor sculptile* ('bust of Columbus', lower left). It is a Mercator cylindrical projection, employing the same maths and resulting in the same type of distortion as the Mercator map of the Earth. The apparent path of the Sun, the ecliptic, is shown across the centre of the map, and the path of the long-period Great Comet of 1807 is shown as a dotted line in the upper right quadrant.

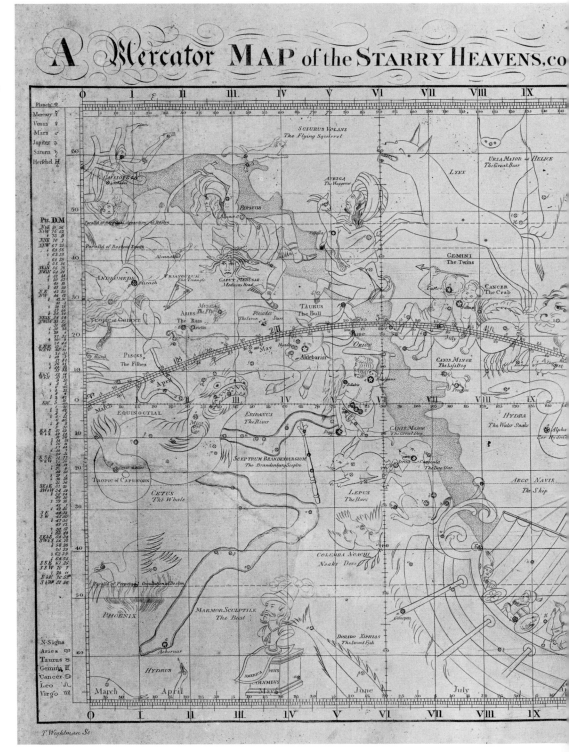

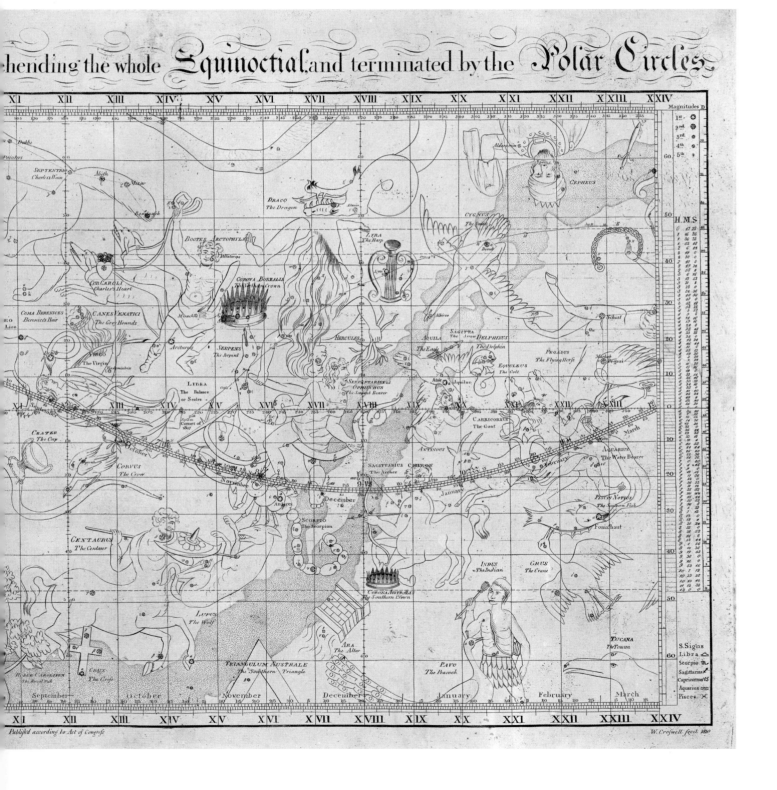

URANIA'S MIRROR, 1825

Urania's Mirror, published in London in 1825, presents beautiful
and clear illustrations of the constellations on a set of 32 printed
cards, possibly intended for the Christmas market. They cost £1 4s
monochrome or £1 18s coloured. The engraver was Sidney Hall, but the
illustrator was credited only as 'a lady' (which may or may not have been
true). The cards were accompanied by a book, *A Familiar Treatise on
Astronomy* by Jehoshaphat Aspin. The pictures are copied almost exactly
from the *Celestial Atlas* of Alexander Jamieson, published in 1823, itself
inspired by Bode's *Uranographia*. The first edition included only the
stars that made up the featured constellations, but a second edition
included surrounding stars. The dotted lines splitting up constellations
were not accepted as the official divisions at this point. These were
introduced in 1930 and have straight edges. The cards were perforated
at the centres of the brightest stars so that if held up to the light the
patterns of the constellations could be seen.

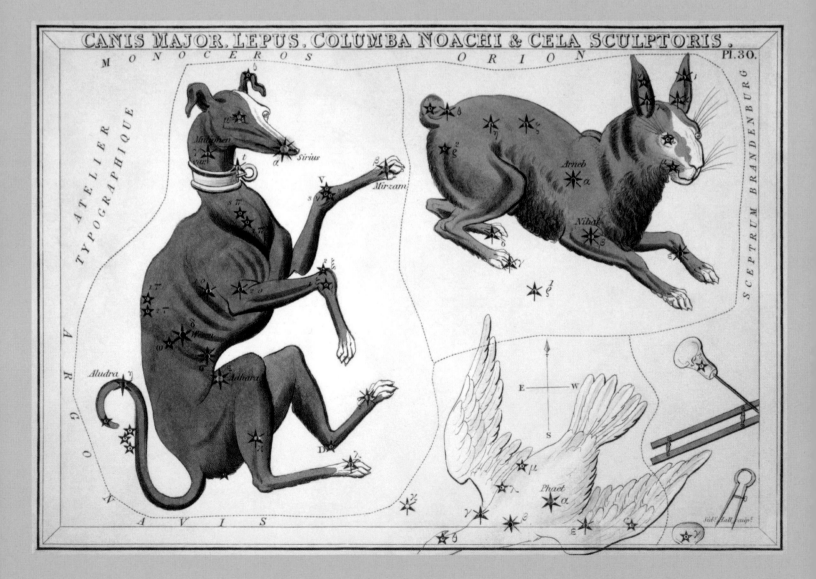

ELIJAH H. BURRITT, THE CONSTELLATIONS, 1856

This image was engraved by W.G. Evans of New York for the 1856 edition of the *Atlas, Designed to Illustrate the Geography of the Heavens* by Elijah Burritt and F.J. Huntington. The atlas, produced for around 20 years from the 1830s to the 1850s, was the most important American celestial geography of the time. It consisted of eight charts, showing the night sky in different seasons in both hemispheres. Many of the names developed for the constellations in the southern hemisphere are still in use.

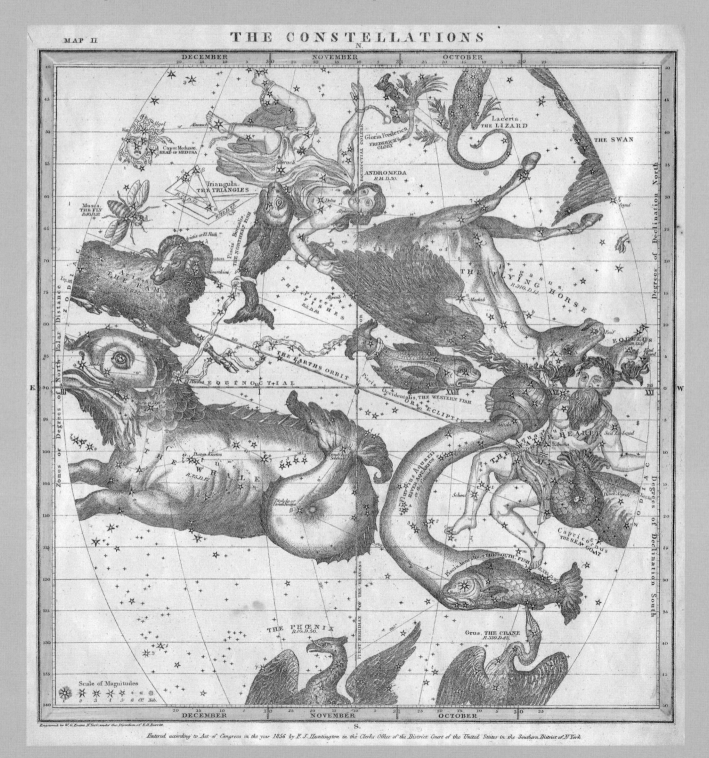

PHILIP'S PLANISPHERE, 1887

This planisphere, introduced by George Philip & Son of London, is a map of the stars visible in the northern hemisphere. A window above the map can be moved to show the stars that will be visible at any particular time during the year. Such a planisphere must be used at the right latitude to be accurate. Instruments like this, mass produced in the late 19th and early 20th centuries, put amateur astronomy within everyone's reach.

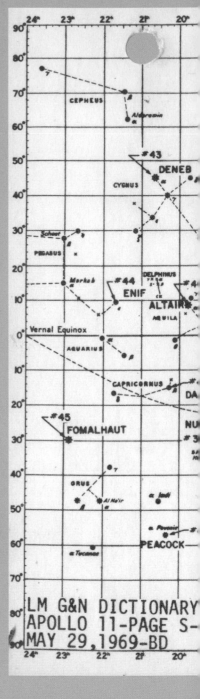

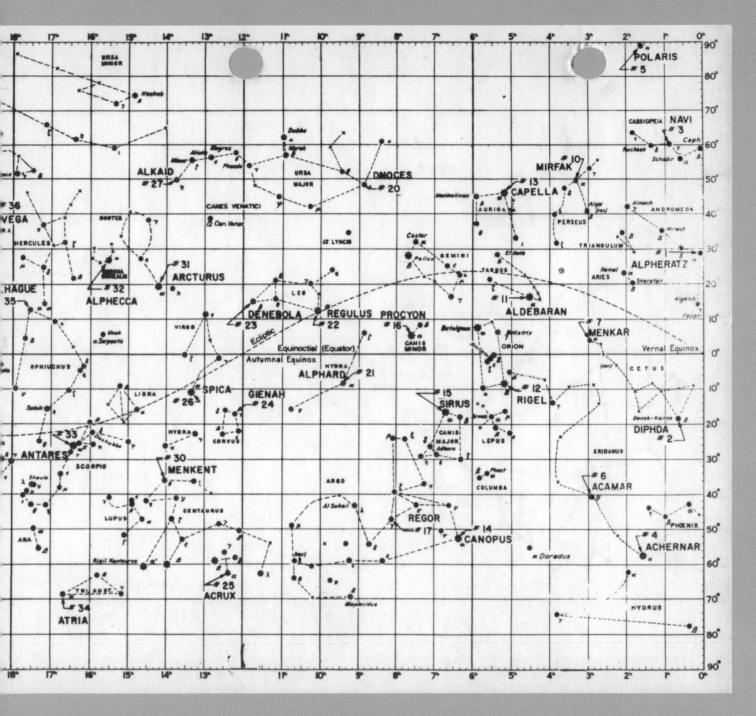

APOLLO 11, FLOWN VERSION OF STAR MAP, 1969

It might look like a scrappy map of the main constellations around the ecliptic, but it's actually the map taken by the Apollo 11 team to navigate to the Moon in 1969. Confusing background stars have been missed out. So has the Moon because its position in relation to the stars would be constantly changing.

The spacecraft did also have a computer, the Apollo Guidance Computer, but it didn't use this to navigate to the Moon. With only 2K RAM and 36K ROM, the Guidance Computer had less computing power and memory than a modern greetings card that plays a tune.

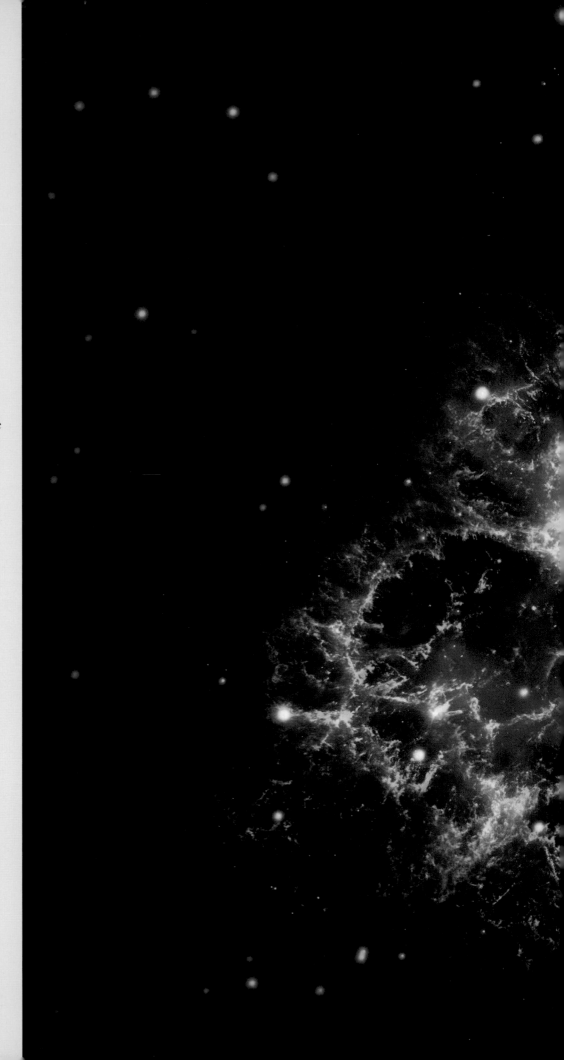

NASA, CRAB
NEBULA (SN 1054),
2017

This composite image of the
Crab Nebula, a supernova
remnant, was assembled by
combining data from five
telescopes spanning nearly
the entire breadth of the
electromagnetic spectrum.
The nebula formed around
7,500 years ago, the results of
a supernova event witnessed
by Chinese and Japanese
astronomers in 1054. This
wispy and filamentary cloud
of gas and dust is found in the
constellation of Taurus, 6,500
light years away from Earth.

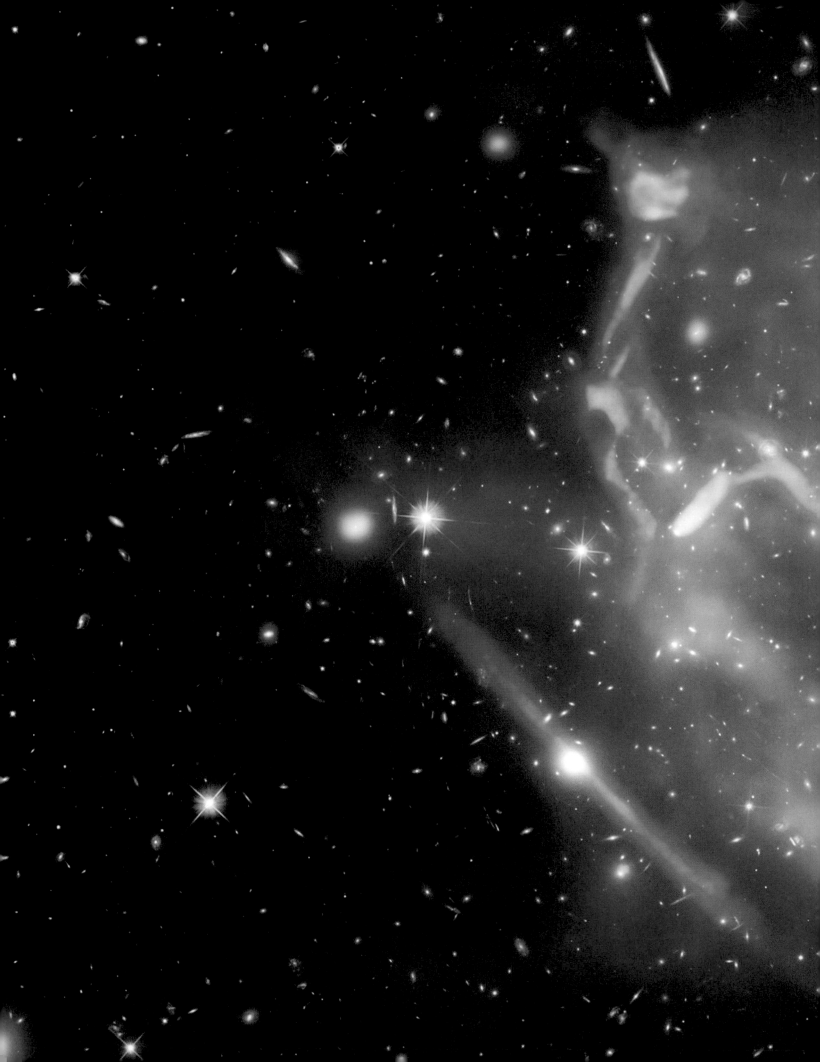

INFINITY AND BEYOND

TO THE EDGE OF THE UNIVERSE

THE PTOLEMAIC MODEL OF THE COSMOS KEPT the heavens neatly contained within a set of nested spheres, but when it was finally challenged, the stars were able to escape, potentially scattering across an infinite void. As the centuries have passed, astronomers have found not only that the stars extend far beyond anything early imagination could conceive, but that our own galaxy is one of billions, all with their own billions of stars. Mapping the universe has become an immense task.

A galaxy cluster consists of thousands of galaxies bound together by gravity. MACS J0717, one of the most complex and distorted galaxy clusters known, is the site of a collision between four clusters. It is about 5.4 billion light years away from Earth.

William Gilbert created this map of the universe for his book De Mundo *which was left unpublished at his death in 1603. It finally appeared in print in 1651 (with his drawing of the Moon, see page 48). He rejected the idea of a 'sphere of stars', showing the stars extending off into the distance, outside the solar system.*

IN A GALAXY FAR, FAR AWAY . . .

Galileo's telescope soon showed that the Milky Way is a band of stars too many and too distant to be distinguished with the naked eye. Later, other galaxies came into view, though they were not immediately recognized as such. When Messier catalogued his 'nebulous objects' (see page 124), he had no idea that some of the objects he had collected lay outside the Milky Way.

The galaxy NGC 1569 was first noted by William Herschel in 1788. It is relatively close and bright, being around 11 million light years away, making it visible to Herschel's telescopes.

The idea that there could be further galaxies had been proposed in 1750 by Thomas Wright, but did not gain traction until the 19th century, and was hotly debated until the question was finally resolved in 1929 by American astronomer Edward Hubble. Using a powerful telescope he was able to pick out individual stars in the Andromeda galaxy and calculate their distance from the Sun. The answer he came up with was a million light years – much farther than the most remote objects within the Milky Way. Astronomers now gather electromagnetic radiation that set out on its journey near the start of the universe, over 13 billion years ago, and use its patterns to help, at last, map the entire universe.

The Fireworks Galaxy (NGC 6946), on the edge of the constellation of Cygnus. This is a composite image from photographs taken by the Japanese Subaru Telescope, National Astronomical Observatory of Japan.

Chapter Six

MAYAN MILKY WAY GLOBE, AD200–500

This Mayan bowl, made in Guatemala between AD200 and 500, depicts the swirl of the Milky Way as a cosmic snake. The Mayans considered the Milky Way to be the path to the otherworld. The carved and blank areas of the bowl represent the perpetual conflict between light and dark, and between this world and the otherworld. The carved portions are filled with animals found in the otherworld and celestial signs.

THOMAS DIGGES, THE INFINITE UNIVERSE, 1576

English astronomer Thomas Digges (*c*.1546–95) wrote a treatise in English called *A Perfit Description of the Caelestiall Orbes according to the most aunciente doctrine of the Pythagoreans, latelye revived by Copernicus and by Geometricall Demonstrations approved*. It included this map and was the first account of the Copernican heliocentric universe in English. Digges went beyond Copernicus in discarding the outer sphere of fixed stars and proposing an infinite universe in which the stars extend outwards into space without end. This was the first statement of an infinite universe since the Ancient Greek philosophers had discussed the possibility in the 5th century BC.

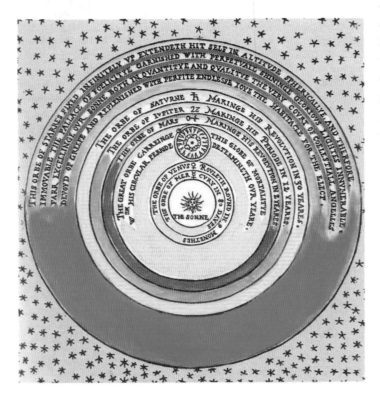

The text around the edge reads: 'This orbe of starres fixed infinitely up extendeth hit self in altitude sphericallye, and therefore immovable the pallace of foelicitye garnished with perpetuall shininge glorious lightes innumerable, farr excelling our sonne both in quantitye and qualitye the very court of coelestiall angelles devoyd of greefe and replenished with perfite endlesse joye the habitacle for the elect.'

THOMAS WRIGHT, MULTIPLE GALAXIES, *AN ORIGINAL THEORY OF THE UNIVERSE*, 1750

The English astronomer Thomas Wright was the first to suggest that the Milky Way is a disc of stars and that we are in the midst of it. He went further, proposing the 'original theory' that the Milky Way is just one of several self-contained galaxies, and even that some of the nebulous objects seen in the night sky might be distant galaxies outside our own: 'the many cloudy spots, just perceivable by us . . . in all likelihood may be external creations, bordering upon the known one, too remote for even our telescopes to reach.'

Of the Milky Way, Wright wrote: 'To a Spectator placed in an indefinite Space, all very remote Objects appear to be equally distant from the Eye; and if we judge of the Via Lactea [Milky Way] from Phaeonmena only, we must of course conclude it is a vast Ring of Stars, scattered promiscuously round the celestial Regions in the Direction of a perfect Circle.'

He suggested a structure for the Milky Way, shown on the right: 'imagine a vast infinite Gulph, or Medium, every Way extended like a Plane, and inclosed between two Surfaces, nearly even on both Sides, but of such a Depth or Thickness as to occupy a Space equal to the double Radius, or Diameter of the visible Creation.'

Wright's radical new model influenced William Herschel and the philosopher Immanuel Kant, but it would be the best part of 200 years before the existence of other galaxies was widely accepted.

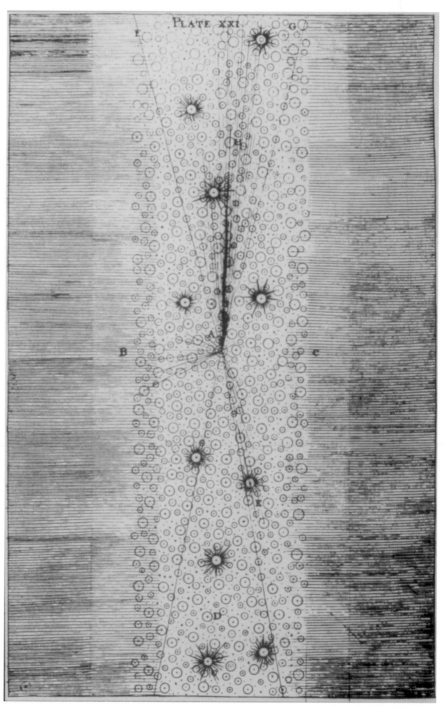

EDWIN DUNKIN, MILKY WAY, 1869

The English astronomer Edwin Dunkin's most famous work was a popular textbook of astronomy called *The Midnight Sky*. A meticulous observer, he based it on his own measurements and records. His book included images of the Milky Way drawn from different places around the Earth and at different times, building up as full a picture as possible of it. This image is of the Milky Way over the Greenwich Observatory in London on 15 August 1869. (The Milky Way is no longer visible over London as light pollution obscures it entirely.)

Dunkin was aware that the Milky Way is a band of stars and the solar system is within it, but as yet there was no consensus as to whether there was anything outside the Milky Way. Dunkin sought to describe the Milky Way, with its twists and gaps and its extravagant density of stars, but did not try to explain it:

'This very remarkable nebulosity extends over a vast portion of the celestial sphere, diverging, at a certain point, into two branches, which afterwards re-unite. To the eye it has the general appearance of a diffused milky light, but of variable intensity. When viewed, however, with a very powerful telescope, it is seen to consist of innumerable stars, so crowded together, at such immense distances from us, that their combined light only produces to the naked eye that nebulous appearance by which it is distinguished. . . . The multitude of minute objects seen in the Milky Way . . . is one of the most marvellous exhibitions of stellar glory with which we are acquainted. On such occasions the stars are scattered over the field of view like glittering dust on the dark ground of the sky.'

THE MIDNIGHT SKY AT LONDON, LOOKING NORTH, DECEMBER 15.

(Available for January 15 at 10 p.m. and February 15 at 8 p.m.)

INDEX-MAP.

FLAMMARION ENGRAVING, 1888

This engraving was made to illustrate a novel by Camille Flammarion, *L'atmosphère: météorologie populaire* (*The Atmosphere: Popular Meteorology*). In it, a missionary of the Middle Ages finds a place where the firmament is not properly fastened to the horizon; he can peel it back and see the mechanical workings of the universe behind it. The image has sometimes been reproduced (often cropped) as a piece of medieval work. It is also used to illustrate the impact of the scientific revolution, when the operation of the universe following physical laws began to challenge explanations based in divinity and the supernatural.

VINCENT VAN GOGH, *THE STARRY NIGHT*, 1889

The Dutch painter Vincent van Gogh depicted the night sky outside the east-facing window of the asylum in which he was incarcerated in Provence, France, in 1889. It has been suggested on several occasions that the swirls of the sky resemble the engraving of the spiral Windmill Galaxy that had been produced 30 years earlier by the Irish astronomer Lord Rosse. Van Gogh probably knew the image through Flammarion's portrayal of it in his popular astronomy books. Rosse was the first to point out the spiral shape of the object (which was not then known to be another galaxy). The Windmill Galaxy is not visible to the naked eye; van Gogh's vision lends a telescopic perspective, recalling the same technique used by Donato Creti around 175 years earlier (see page 96).

Rosse produced his engraving of the object now known as the Whirlpool Galaxy in 1850.

NASA, ANTENNAE GALAXIES, 2013

Two galaxies slowly rewriting the map of the universe are the colliding Antennae Galaxies, NGC 4038 and NGC 4039, 65 million light years away. The two galaxies have been tangled in a gravity-driven battle, tearing each other apart, for hundreds of millions of years. Vast clouds of dust and gas are shown here in pink and red; blue areas are regions of intense star-forming activity. Stars torn out of the two galaxies form long streamers extending into space and joining the two galaxies. The galaxies are in a storm of star creation called a starburst, with all the gas within the galaxies being poured into the generation of new stars. Eventually, the two will lose their separate identities and merge into a single elliptical galaxy.

The image here was created from recent visible and near-infrared data from the Hubble Space Telescope, combined with some older information. As the galaxies are 65 million light years away, the image shows them in the state they were in at the time of the extinction of the dinosaurs on Earth – they will have made some progress towards coalescence since then.

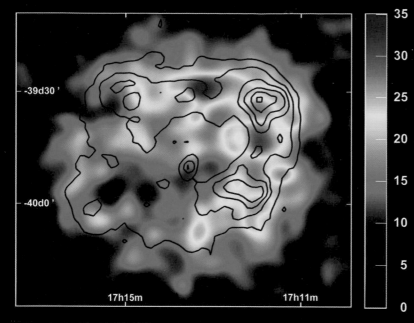

NASA, SUPERNOVA REMNANT, 2004

While some of the nebulous objects identified by Messier are galaxies, others are supernova remnants. Those he saw were all within the Milky Way, but with modern telescopes it is also possible to see supernovae in other galaxies, though in less detail. A supernova remnant within the Milky Way (so, relatively nearby) can look around the same size as an entire distant galaxy.

Although Messier could record the position and shape of supernovae, he could do no more, while modern techniques allow sophisticated mapping of them. The image above shows the intensity of gamma rays emitted by a supernova remnant located near the constellation Scorpio. Supernova remnants are the expanding clouds of gas and dust produced by the collapse of a star and subsequent expulsion of all its matter. Gamma rays are a very high-energy form of radiation and difficult to measure, but this map successfully shows that supernovae emit them at high intensity and supports the idea that they are sources of cosmic rays. Red regions indicate areas of the highest intensity of gamma-ray emission, with blue areas the lowest level. The black contour lines indicate patterns of intensity of X-ray emission. The remnant, with the cumbersome name RXJ1713.7-3946, is possibly the remains of a supernova recorded by Chinese astronomers in AD393. This supernova remnant was not visible to Messier, being too faint for his telescopes.

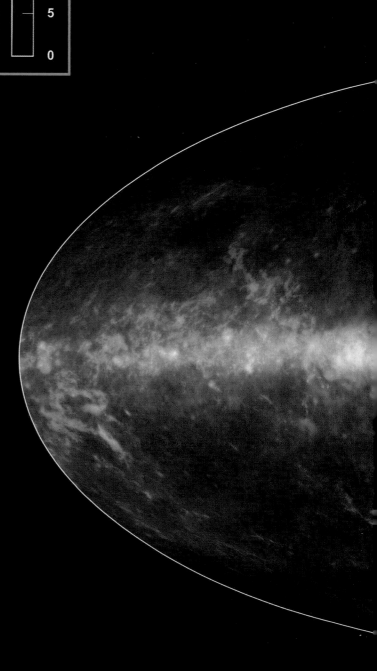

ESA, MILKY WAY, 2009–13

This map of the Milky Way was produced by Planck, a European Space Agency mission launched in 2009. It shows the concentrations of gas, charged particles and dust that make up the Milky Way and is pieced together from maps of the cosmic background radiation which was produced near the birth of the universe.

Different colours in the image represent different materials and types of radiation. Red shows dust that gives off heat. Yellow represents carbon monoxide, concentrated in dense clouds of gas and dust that are producing new stars. Blue and green show different types of radiation. Blue is synchrotron radiation, produced by fast-moving electrons such as those produced by supernovae. The electrons are travelling along the magnetic field of the Milky Way close to the speed of light. Green is radiation produced by electrons and protons that almost collide, slowing down as they approach. They are found in hot, ionized gas clouds near massive stars.

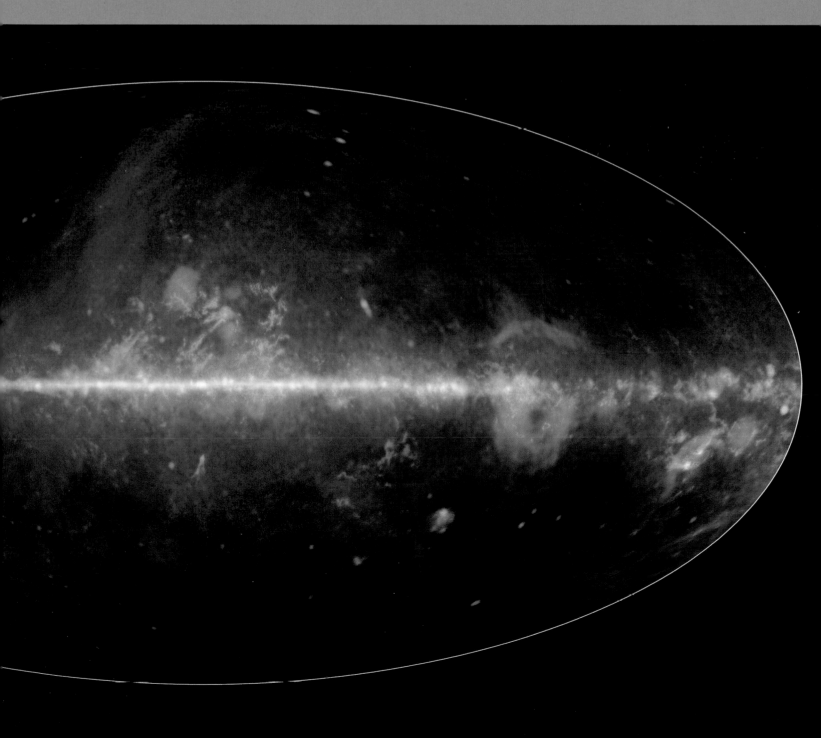

ESA, ENTIRE UNIVERSE, 2015

This image, created from data collected by the European
Space Agency's Planck space observatory, shows the
distribution of matter through the entire visible universe –
from Earth to the outer edge. The areas with more mass
are light-coloured, and areas with less mass are dark blue.
The areas shaded in grey across the middle of the image
are obscured by light from our own galaxy, preventing the
collection of data from distant space.

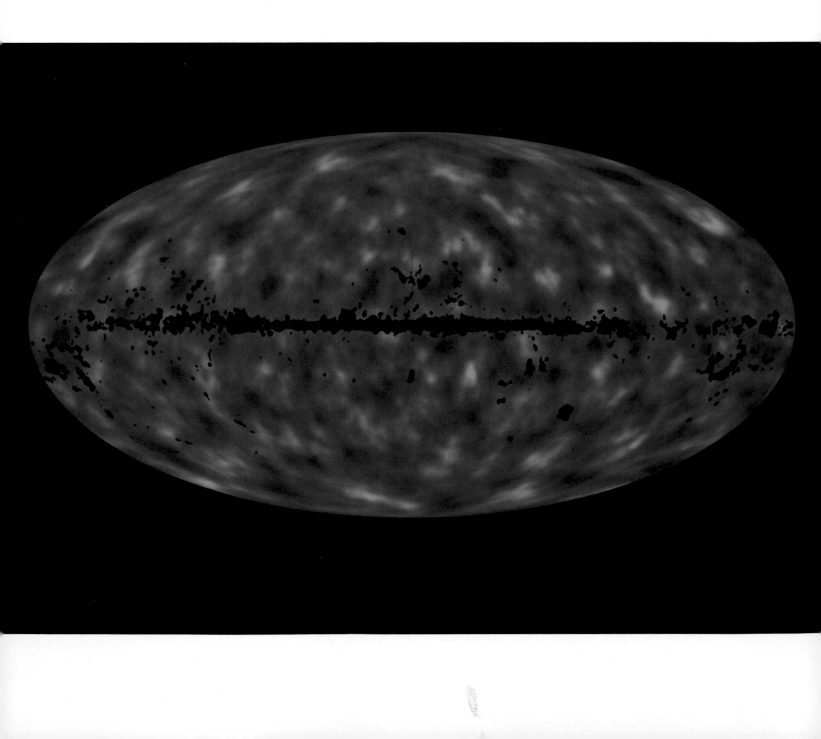

INDEX

PICTURE CREDITS

AKG Images: 96 (Rabatti & Domingie); **Alamy Stock Photo:** 12 (Photo Researchers, Inc.), 13 (Pictorial Press Ltd.), 21 (Science History Images), 114 (Science History Images), 121 (World History Archive), 122–3 (Science History Images), 138 top (Paul Fearn), 163, 185 (Science History Images); **Bridgeman Image Library:** 11, 24–5, 26, 31, 116, 126, 138–9 bottom, 142–3, 144, 174, 186 top; **California Map Society:** 42–3; **Digital Museum of Planetary Mapping:** 58, 59 top, 60; **Diomedia:** 100 bottom (Stockrek Images), 130 (Photononstop/Patrick Somelet), 145 (Wellcome Images CC), 160 top (De Agostini), 164 (Heritage Images), 165 (Heritage Images); **European Space Agency:** 125 bottom, 128–9 (Hubble & NASA), 188–9; **Getty Images:** 9 (Universal Images Group), 16 (Bettmann), 29, 34–5 (Universal Images Group), 38–9 (De Agostini), 53 (De Agostini), 62 top, 90 (DEA/A. Dagli Orti), 124 (Corbis/VCG), 136 (UIG), 137 (UIG), 150 top (De Agostini), 151 (UIG), 184 (SSPL/Science Museum); **Google Earth:** 92–3; **Hubble Space Telescope:** 181, 187; P. Frankenstein/H. Zwietasch; **Landesmuseum Wurttemberg, Stuttgart:** 134; **Mary Evans Picture Library:** 115 top; **Metropolitan Museum of Art, New York:** 54–5, 63; **NASA:** 46–7, 66, 67, 68 (Goddard Space Flight Center/DLR/ASU), 69, 74–5, 76 (JHUAPL/SwRI), 80 (Johns Hopkins University Applied Physics Laboratory/Carnegie Institution of Washington), 81x2 (Johns Hopkins University Applied Physics Laboratory/Carnegie Institution of Washington), 87x2, 95 top, 110–111, 113 top, 133 bottom, 175, 176–7, 178–9, 180 bottom, 188 top; **New York Public Library:** 183 top; **Science & Society Picture Library:** 51 (NASA); **Science Photo Library:** 22, 23 (Library of Congress, Geography and Map Division), 27 (Library of Congress), 28 (Library of Congress), 30, 52 top, 59 bottom (Royal Astronomical Society), 61 (American Philosophical Society), 70–71 (Dr A.W. Grossman et al), 73, 78 (Royal Astronomical Society), 79 (US Geological Survey), 82 (Science Source), 83 (Library of Congress), 89 (Detlev van Ravenswaay), 91 (Royal Astronomical Society), 98–9 (Damian Peach), 100 top (NASA/JPL/Space Science Institute), 102 (European Southern Observatory/L. Fletcher), 104 top (Universal History Archive/UIG), 108 top (Royal Astronomical Society), 112 (Detlev van Ravenswaay), 118 (Library of Congress), 119 (Humanities and Social Sciences Library/Rare Books Division/New York Public Library), 120 (Science Source), 127 (European Space Agency/Rosetta/MPS for Osiris Team MPS/UPD/LAM/IAA/SSO/INTA/UPM/DASP/IDA), 147 bottom (Royal Astronomical Society), 167, 168 (United States Naval Observatory), 170–171 (Library of Congress, Geography and Map Division), 183 bottom, 190–191 (ESA/NASA/JPL-Caltech); **Shutterstock:** 6–7, 10, 14–15, 77; **Topham Picturepoint:** 148 (Charles Walker), 149 (Charles Walker), 160 bottom (Alinari); **University of Manchester:** 117x2; **Wellcome Library, London:** 113 bottom.

Diagram on page 50 by David Woodroffe